T0065524

IT IS POSSIBLE

IT IS POSSIBLE

Experience the Abundant Life

Galen Swanigan

WestBow Press books may be ordered through booksellers or by contacting:

WestBow Press
A Division of Thomas Nelson & Zondervan
1663 Liberty Drive
Bloomington, IN 47403
www.westbowpress.com
844-714-3454

ISBN: 978-1-6642-1970-0 (sc)
ISBN: 978-1-6642-1972-4 (hc)
ISBN: 978-1-6642-1971-7 (e)

Library of Congress Control Number: 2021901757

Print information available on the last page.

WestBow Press rev. date: 01/29/2021

Contents

Acknowledgements

I want to take this opportunity to thank some very special people in my life. Their presence has truly been instrumental in enabling me to live an abundant life. First, I want to thank my wife Elaine for her love and encouragement. We have been married forty-three years and through all that time she has been the shining example of the Godly woman described in Proverbs 31. "Love you E." Next, our children who have shown love and mercy to me when I have been less than my best and have provided a richness of life experience which cannot be overstated. My mother and grandparents who provided an environment which encouraged me to follow God with all my heart. My father-in-law and mother-in-law who modeled Christ in action to all with whom they came in contact. Dear friends have been by my side in the good and not so good times and lived out the love of God in a tangible way. They have blessed my life more than I can express. Spiritual mentors, pastors, and Sunday School teachers who have provided Godly insight and a gentle nudge for me to step up my game. I do not know where my life would be without these individuals to help point me to God.

I want to thank the individuals who gave up their time to read through the draft of this book and provided valuable insight into what needed work and to those who have worked on copy editing, book covers, and all the incredibly important behind the scenes work that has to happen. Thank you!

I want to thank Rod Handley for providing encouragement to pursue this endeavor and for sharing his expertise as to how the process of writing a book really works.

Lastly, I must thank my Lord and Savior Jesus Christ for paying the penalty for my sin and making possible a life which can be abundantly lived.

Introduction

I felt compelled to write this book because I wanted to have something which could be handed down to my wonderful children, grandchildren, and future generations. I wanted them to have a picture of what has helped me (Dad and Grandpa/Gramps) to view life in realistic terms and what has helped me make decisions as I have walked through life. I felt it vital to communicate how importantly I value my relationship with God and to express my reliance on God as my source of strength in all areas of my life.

I pray those who come after me will become followers of Jesus Christ, and they will allow Jesus to reveal to them what an abundant life can look like. I pray they will apply God's knowledge and wisdom to their lives so they will be able to experience and live out the abundant life God has for them, and to live in such a fashion for all their days on this earth. I hope all who read this book will examine their relationship with God and allow Him to guide them as they walk through their own life journey.

Over the course of my life, I have had the opportunity to observe different frames of reference for how people live their lives. Some believe their life is made up entirely of what they experience and do. Some believe there is a flow of the universe, and they strive to fit into that flow. Some believe they are a result of their environment and therefore have limited ability to change their behavior. I appreciate some nuances of each of these perspectives.

I believe the universe in which I exist was made by God, the creator. He knows best how I am made, and He knows the best course of action for me to take as I journey through my life on this earth. I have found the concepts and principles which are given to me in the Bible to be true.

While being in corporate America for more than four decades I had the opportunity to experience many different training and education programs concerning how to work with, influence and be a leader of people. In each of these programs the concepts being presented had their roots in what is taught in the Holy Bible. Knowing ourselves, treating others with respect, seeking and applying wisdom, and following through on our commitments are all concepts taught in God's word.

If I accept the view that I am part of God's creation, then I believe I would be wise to strive to understand those concepts and attempt to live them out to the best of my ability. I am sixty-seven years old, and I realize now more than ever that life is very fleeting. I understand better every day that I do not know what my life will be like tomorrow. The Bible says we are like a vapor which appears for a little while and then vanishes (*New International Version*, James 4:14). Life is too short to spend it living a mediocre existence when God has promised us something else. While we seem to have all the time in the world, time does have a way of marching on. I want to make the most of the time I am given and use the blessing of time to the glory of God.

We find the following passage in scripture; "The thief comes only to steal and kill and destroy; I have come that they may have life, and have it to the full" (John 10:10) I have certainly found this biblical statement to be true in my life. When I follow a standard of conduct which does not match up to scriptural instruction, the results do not turn out so well. When I follow the standards which God has given me, things just seem to go better. I want to pass this important learning on to others.

This book is not about earning salvation because God's word clearly states we cannot earn our position with God. We are told this, "For it is by grace you have been saved, through faith—and this is not from yourselves, it is the gift of God" (Ephesians 2:8). Some of the more familiar scriptures which speak to this concept are Galatians 2:16, Romans 4:3, and 2 Corinthians 5:21. We are told we are unclean and our own righteousness is like filthy rags (Isaiah 64:6). Left to our own devices we would never be able to cleanse ourselves.

Many of the most fulfilled people I have been blessed to meet in life were not rich by earthly standards; they may have had health issues which were severe and eventually took their lives, and they may not have been individuals to whose door the world would beat a path for the latest worldly wisdom. They were, however, people who trusted God to walk with them each step of the way and they exhibited grace and peace to everyone they encountered. Even though many of those people are now in Heaven, the example of the way they lived their lives still impacts me today. The ripple effects go on and on.

I have been trying to follow Christ for the last fifty-eight years of my life, and for more than half a century I have found Him to be faithful in all situations. He has forgiven and continues to forgive me when I confess that I have fallen short of doing His will. He has comforted me when I have been confronted with struggles which overwhelm my ability to understand. He has provided guidance when there were multiple choices which could be made, and I did not know which one was best. He has provided peace when the report from the doctor said cancer. These are just snapshots of some of the times He has been by my side in my journey on this earth. In all these situations and many more, I have found it is because of the marvelous grace and mercy of our creator God that I am able to move forward.

My belief is that I am not unique in life. If we live long enough, each of us will be confronted with events and situations which are beyond our ability to manage in our own strength. God's word speaks to this concept in the words of Jesus: "I have told you these things, so that in me you may have peace. In this world you will have trouble. But take heart! I have overcome the world" (John 16:33). Just because we are Christ followers, we are not exempt from issues. The following verses also speak to that reality: James 1:2–4, and 1 Thessalonians 3:2–4. All these scriptures tell us we will experience trials. Trials are a part of the human condition.

The reality is that our inheritance is in Heaven and not here on earth. We can greatly rejoice in the fact that we have the promise of being with Jesus in Heaven. "Praise be to the God and Father of our Lord Jesus Christ! In His great mercy He has given us new birth into a living hope through the resurrection of Jesus Christ from the dead, and into an inheritance which can never perish, spoil, or fade. This inheritance is kept in heaven for you, who through faith are shielded by God's power until the coming of the salvation that is ready to be revealed in the last time. In all this you greatly rejoice, though now for a little while you may have had to suffer grief in all kinds of trials. These have come so that the proven genuineness of your faith—of greater worth than gold, which perishes even though refined by fire—may result in praise, glory and honor when Jesus Christ is revealed" (1 Peter 1:3–7). When I realize this earth is not the final chapter in my story, I am freed to focus on what will last. I can be assured I will be with Jesus Christ in Heaven.

I want us to explore some of the attributes of professing Christians who seemingly come through every situation they face with peace and victory. What is it that enables these individuals to accomplish what would otherwise seem difficult, if not impossible? You see, every Christian has the availability of God's word which can be used to guide his or her life. We all have the option of leaning on God's word as we journey through this life on earth. Yet it seems there are those who are always 'PLUMs,' and dwell on 'poor little unfortunate me.' Jesus has promised us so much more than a PLUM existence. He has promised us abundant life—life to the full.

We all have the ability to follow the path King David speaks about when he makes the following statement. "I seek you with all my heart; do not let me stray from your commands. I have hidden your word in my heart that I might not sin against you. Praise be to you, Lord; teach me your decrees" (Psalms 119:10–12). Believers in Jesus Christ have the promise that the Holy Spirit of God will abide in us daily. When we seek God, He will teach us His decrees.

Jesus gives us the following promise, "And I will ask the Father, and he will give you another advocate to help you and be with you forever—the Spirit of truth. The world cannot accept him, because it neither sees him nor knows him. But you know him, for he lives with you and will be in you. I will not leave you as orphans; I will come to you" (John 14:16–18). These are strong words from scripture which are given to all of us. Why are there times in my life and the lives of others when we feel defeated and as if we are all alone in our walk? I have found when I have those feelings, I can trust the fact that God loves me and does not condemn me. He gives me a helper and not condemnation.

When I feel I am in the center of God's will, I believe I can point to some definite personal goals and targets I am actively pursuing. They are important priorities, and I treat them as such. I want to be able to look at the target and say that with God's help, my behavior has hit the mark. Conversely, when I do not focus on those goals and targets, it is easy for me to become distracted and give the devil room for encroachment into my life. When this happens, my life seems to be out of sync with what I really want to achieve. In those times of being out of sync, I ask for God's Holy Spirit to minister to me.

In this book we will look at what scripture has to say about the will of God. We will also examine what Jesus said are behaviors which accompany being blessed. We are going to explore the importance of setting personal goals and targets for our lives, and areas in which we need to take personal responsibility for the achievement of certain goals. We will explore the lives of some Biblical characters and see how their goals impacted their decisions.

I pray God will give all of us wisdom as we explore the importance of having the correct set of goals for our life and that God will show each of us what our responsibility is in accomplishing those goals. Lastly, I pray we will allow God's spirit to guide and empower us to live a life which is 'on target' for Jesus Christ during our time in this world. I believe a life well lived will influence others to look to Jesus Christ as their own personal savior.

Thoughts to Consider

- Do I view each day as an opportunity for fulfillment or as a trial to get through?
- Am I a person who naturally takes responsibility for my actions?
- Do I see myself as having unique circumstances to face?
- Do I believe there is a correlation between my behaviors and my experiences?
- Do my behaviors determine my experiences or do my experiences determine my behaviors?
- What are the things I want to accomplish with my life?
- Do I want to live triumphantly?
- Am I open to what God's word has to say about the abundant life?

The Battle Starts in Our Minds

One of the most important things I have come to realize in my life is that I must address any issue I am trying to solve, any habit I am trying to establish, or any skill I am trying to learn by first getting my mind in the right place. Sometimes this means reprogramming my mind, for this is the only way in which true change is going to happen. If I am totally locked in on the idea that I know what is best, at a minimum, I do not expand my ideas to include something which might help me improve. I do not try another approach to the situation and thus get the same results.

Over our lifetimes there are innumerable sources feeding into our minds, influencing how we think. Not all these sources will help us accomplish what God would have us do. The earliest sources feeding our minds come from our family of origin. It is in the home environment we learn if it is safe to explore our world; we learn to ask questions and try new things.

I had the advantage of growing up in a rural environment around tractors, cars, trucks, chainsaws, and other cool stuff. My father would let me use any of the equipment if he was confident I would follow his instruction to the letter. He would then show me how to operate the equipment and make sure I was big enough to use the controls in a safe manner. When I look back at those years, it was a great way for me to learn what works and sometimes after a few cuts, bumps and bruises, what doesn't work. All those experiences helped shape my thinking.

We also make our journey through the education system. Here we learn how to acquire information, how to synthesize it and store it in our minds. We learn what it is like to stand out or to go along with the crowd. We have our first attempts at navigating relationships outside of our family. All these events are sources which feed into our minds.

We start the work phase of our lives and learn what it means to balance what we want to do with what we have to do. We learn what it means to be in situations where we are praised or cursed and sometimes both at the same time. We learn we cannot trust everyone, and we experience the fact that not everyone thinks or looks like we do.

Most of us have social connections with others as we go through life. Some of us attend houses of worship where we feed the spiritual part of our existence. We may belong to teams, clubs, professional organizations, or unions. We learn what people place value in and how we fit into those organizations.

All our past experiences are taken in by our minds and shape how we view our past, what we think we can accomplish in the present, and what we want to aim for in the future. Art Markman, Ph.D., cognitive scientist at the University of Texas, posted a paper on August 12, 2011, for Psychology Today that provides background concerning how we form habits. In his article Dr. Markman referenced a paper in the August 2011 issue of Memory and Cognition by Kathleen Arnold, Kathleen McDermott, and Karl Szpunar. This article pointed out the following: Our ability to envision the future is strongly influenced by our past memory. We use those experiences and memories to form an image of what we believe the future will be like. We then use those images of the future to help us make plans. In an article "On Being 'Triggered': How Emotional Memories Affect Us," by Mary C. Lamia, PhD, published on November 11,2017, we are told the following: "Emotional memories are powerful.

They serve to guide and inform us as we navigate through the present and prepare for the future." This statement shows there is a direct connection between our past experiences and how we perceive the present. What is in our mind is important because we are impacted by the knowledge we have stored there.

It is important for us to actively allow God to help get our minds in the right place. Paul instructed us to not conform to the world's patterns but to renew our minds (Romans 12:1–2). This means we are to think differently than the world's view of how to address things, and we are to look at our situation from the perspective which God's word brings to bear. God's word is the primary source of what we need to avail ourselves in order to get our minds in the right spot.

We are instructed to take all our thoughts and have them be obedient to the teachings of Christ (2 Corinthians 10:5) . This scripture implies we must take an active role in aligning our thoughts and minds with the teaching of Christ. We are told to control our thoughts and not let them control us. Controlling our thoughts is more than just positive thinking; it is about developing a whole new way to process information and come to a conclusion.

Let's examine two scriptures which provide guidance as to how we are to put the teachings of God into our minds. We are told to meditate on God's law and delight in the law of the Lord (Joshua 1:8 and Psalms 1:1–2). When we examine those directives, it is easy to say, "OK, I can do it." These scriptures provide the next step in the process of getting God's word into our minds; We are told we are to meditate on God's law, day and night.

In Richard J. Foster's book *Celebration of Discipline The Path to Spiritual Growth*, HarperCollins Publishers, 1998. p 15, we are given words used to convey the idea of meditation. These words have various meanings which include listening to God's word, reflecting on God's works, rehearsing God's deeds, ruminating on God's law, and more. The purpose of meditation is to help bring about changed behavior because we have encountered God. The actions we undertake in meditation help bring about the following: "We create an emotional and spiritual space which allows Christ to construct an inner sanctuary in the heart" p 20.

Jesus tells us if the evil man has evil thoughts in his heart, those thoughts will bring about evil. The good man has good treasure in his heart and his heart brings forth what is good (Luke 6:45) . Jesus tells us it is out of our heart that our mouth speaks. Is it any wonder followers of Christ are told to think about what is true, honorable, right, pure, lovely, admirable, excellent, and anything worthy of praise (Philippians 4:8–9 NLT)? These are the things we are to put into the emotional and spiritual space which is created when we meditate on God.

This meditation process is more than simply checking off a box called daily devotion or daily reading of scripture and then going about the rest of our normal business feeling good with ourselves because we have done our duty. This is more than purchasing the latest Christian self-help book and having a book club meeting to recap. This is about taking control of our mind with the purpose of having God's thoughts become our thoughts. This can only be realized at it's fullest when we truly make a conscious decision to meditate on God's word. There are no shortcuts.

We are told to submit ourselves to God and resist the devil (James 4:7). The rest of the verse tells us that when we do those things, the devil will flee from us. I have found this scripture to be very meaningful and helpful. For me this is an example of taking control of my mind so God's thoughts—His instructions to me—can be at the front of my mind and then influence my actions.

The commanded behavior of meditating day and night must become a way of life if we want to live an abundant life for Christ. Meditating day and night programs our minds and hearts to apply the wisdom and commands of God to our motives and actions. I have found when I follow these concepts (renewing my mind, keeping my thoughts captive and under control, and meditating on God's instruction), my mind is opened to the wisdom and instruction which God can bring into my consciousness concerning the issues I face, habits I am learning or unlearning, and any new skill I am attempting. God's word is clear—it starts in the mind.

In the mid 1980's my wife and I were privileged to become involved in Nazarene Marriage Enrichment. We felt impressed by the Holy Spirit that this was an area of kingdom service in which we needed to be involved. We were privileged to be trained by the couple who developed the program, J. Paul and Marilyn Turner. One day, during a break between sessions, J. Paul came to me and asked, "Galen, do you want to truly be effective for God?" I thought for a brief moment and responded with this statement, "Yes, J. Paul, I want to be used by God." I will never forget J. Paul's next statement: "Then you will need to memorize scripture. It must become a part of you."

What was J. Paul telling me? I believe he was telling me that reading the Bible is a good thing. We must practice this discipline to feed our spiritual souls. However, the word of God must be such a part of us that our minds become reprogrammed so our first thoughts are about pleasing God, and our first response is God-directed. The conversation with J. Paul happened almost 35 years ago, and I must say I have found J. Paul to be one hundred percent correct. There are times we will not have access to a Bible or a Bible app on our phones (I do love those apps). We must have God's word in our minds.

In one of the jobs I held with my former employer, I worked in a group which supported desktop publishing technology. This was in the late 1980's. The support included software (most of which was beta, total custom, or in-house developed), hardware (printers, scanners, monitors, etc.), and custom-developed workflow application support. Our group supported about fifty creative and graphic art process workstations. We also supported the group which developed the custom-made software and processes.

The development group was notorious for doing what we called the Friday Dump, which meant making changes to existing systems or even making new systems and then putting those systems out to the users right before everyone went home on Friday evening. Guess what happened more times than not? My group would come in on Monday morning to systems which would not work and operators who were, to say the least, very frustrated.

The manager of the development group was brilliant with regard to programming the systems to perform as intended. However, he did not necessarily appreciate our concerns about the Friday Dump. I knew the situation was not going to get better; it was going to get worse. So, I scheduled a meeting with the developers and myself. I was the youngest person in the room and also had the least amount of experience, but...the meeting must go on.

I remember praying before the meeting started that I would be able to think clearly. We all got in the room, and sure enough, it became evident it was going to be difficult to get everyone to a common place of understanding concerning what needed to be changed. I was in the corner of the room and out of nowhere I had the following scripture flash through my mind, "For the Spirit God gave us does not make us timid, but gives us power, love and self-discipline" (2 Timothy 1:7) There could not have been a more appropriate scripture for the situation.

You see, everyone in the room knew I was a religious person. How I acted in the meeting could have a potentially long-lasting impact. I could not be timid. It was my responsibility to address the situation. I needed to be disciplined about how I communicated, and probably most importantly, I needed to exhibit 'love' for the others in the room. By love, I mean I needed to understand the individuals were not trying to be difficult—they had issues to deal with as well—and I needed to attempt to understand their issues (this looks a little like the Beatitude concerning being a peacemaker). How long did it take my mind to process the scripture? Not long at all—maybe a couple of seconds. As a result of this internal process and my resulting actions, from that point forward we were able to make some real headway, and we left the meeting with everyone feeling valued. When I got out of the meeting, I reflected on my earlier conversation with J. Paul and how his words had proven true in real-life. If I wanted to be effective for God, I needed to memorize scripture. I needed to be reprogramming my mind.

Have I always had a scripture come to mind or been able to act appropriately in every situation? I wish I could say yes, but the real answer is no. I do have a strong conviction that God is there to help guide us if we will do the work and then allow Him to have his words and wisdom impact our thoughts and actions. I am convinced that meditating on God's word is critical to our ability to live abundantly for Him.

Thoughts to Consider

- Are there areas in my mind which I have locked to the possibility of change?
- What have I allowed to program my mind?
- What could 'not being conformed to this world' look like for me?
- Do I control my thoughts, or do they control me?
- What does meditation mean to me?
- How can I more fully develop the process of allowing God to renew my mind?

God's Will, Can We Know It?

Over the course of my life I have heard the phrase uttered with great conviction, "It is God's will that..." The next part of the sentence has run the whole gamut of human experience—things like, "I know it is God's will that I take this job, God doesn't want me to be poor;" "It is God's will that I marry this person; they are beautiful;" "It is God's will that I buy that house, it is in a great neighborhood;" "It is God's will that I buy that truck, especially the red one;" "It is God's will that I leave my family; God wants me to be happy;" "It is God's will that I attend this church;" "It is God's will that I take this promotion;" "It is God's will that I retire;" "It is God's will that I write a book;" "It is God's will that I am sick;" "It is God's will that I go to school here;" "It is God's will that I live by the ocean;" "It is God's will that I __________...;" the list seems to go on forever.

Some of these things could in fact be within the overall will of God, but on the other hand, some are obviously not. I am concerned we are sometimes quick to insert our desires in the blank. We then work to convince ourselves the desire we just inserted is 'God's will.' I believe this is especially true for those of us who have grown up in the United States or other western cultures.

We live in a land of great plenty. We would really like to have our 'slice of the pie.' According to Red Crow Marketing, Inc. (redcrowmarketing.com) we are exposed to somewhere between 4,000 and 10,000 advertisements each day. StopAd blog (stopad.io) cites the marketing firm *Yankelovich, Inc.* as saying the average person is exposed to approximately 5,000 ads per day. According to The Business Journals (bizjournals.com) some believe while the multi-thousands of ads per day may be high, the fact remains a lot of people are spending a lot of money to try to convince us we need to spend our money to get what they have to offer. It is almost like we can't help ourselves; we sometime begin to really believe we need what we desire. Whether it be stuff, status, personal gratification, entitlement, or one of my personal favorites 'just because,' we need to be very careful when it comes to the things we strive for, the things we set up as targets. What we set up as our targets become the things which influence and sometimes control our thoughts and actions. Over the course of time we will try to hit those targets and possibly succeed to a lesser or greater degree.

Our objectives, goals, targets, or whatever word we use to describe what we are striving for must be in alignment with God's word. If not, just like the foolish man Jesus described in Matthew 7, the rains will come, the streams will rise and the winds will blow against the house, and the house will fall with a great crash. The great promise we have is God tells us in Proverbs 3:5–6 to "Trust in the Lord with all your heart and lean not on your own understanding; in all your ways submit to him and he will make your paths straight." When we allow God to show us what we need to be aiming for, we can be assured He will not forsake us, and we have peace in the midst of any situation.

A wise person once gave me this advice, "Galen, just because you think something doesn't necessarily make it so. Be careful what you believe and aim for." All our personal goals must be measured against the framework of the Bible. If we claim to be followers of Christ, then we must make sure our personal goals can be supported by what the word of God says. In Proverbs we are given classic comparisons between wisdom and folly, honesty and falsehood, knowledge and mockers, holding our tongue versus being quick tempered and many more core attributes of wisdom. We are provided with invaluable insight into our ability to rationalize our desires and actions. "There is a way that appears to be right, but in the end it leads to death" (Proverbs 14:12). This verse speaks to the importance of setting the correct targets for ourselves. It is possible to shoot for the wrong thing, hit the target, and in the end, it leads to death.

Our overarching goal in life should be to become more like Jesus. We are to strive to be like Christ. Paul tells us in the third chapter of Philippians that he wanted to know Christ, to participate in Christ's sufferings, and become like Christ in Christ's death and resurrection. We are instructed to be holy as God is holy (1 Peter 1:15–17). This goal/target sets a high-level expectation we need to have for ourselves, and it also provides an image of what the Bible sets as the ultimate target for us.

It is appropriate for us to look at some definitions. When we talk about the will of God, we need to know what the word 'will' means. Webster (merriam-webster.com) says this about will, when used as a verb, it is: "to express futurity, to express desire, choice, willingness, consent, or used to express a command, exhortation, or injunction." When used as a noun it means "desire, wish, passion, choice and determination." The phrase "God's will" could be restated like this; God's desire, wish, choice, or His determination and command for me for the future is that I… When we look at this phrase it is more than just a casual suggestion, it speaks to the very reason God wants to interact with us. This phrase would seem to be speaking to the very reason we have life. It would seem life is certainly more important than what we wear or what we eat today. This is getting at the crux of the reason for our time on earth.

Let us look at some of the specific things the Bible says about the will of God. Perhaps the most important thing we need to understand is God is Love and He does not want anyone to perish but have eternal life with Him (John 3:16). Jesus says everyone who looks to the Son and believes in Him shall have eternal life (John 6:30). We can say with certainty that eternal life is the will of God. This is the promise which God has given to us.

In the Old Testament we find what is commonly referred to as the Ten Commandments (Exodus 20). The first four commandments are about how we are to relate to God. These commands are as follows:

- having no other gods before God
- not worshiping idols,
- not taking God's name in vain, and
- honoring the Sabbath day to keep it holy.

The next six commandments set down the rules for how we are to relate to our fellow man. Those commands are:

- honoring our parents so our days may be long on the earth,
- not committing murder,
- not committing adultery,
- not stealing,
- not lying
- not coveting.

These commands were given to the Hebrew children with the expectation they were to be followed regardless of what the Hebrew children thought they should do. These behaviors are part of God's will for our lives as we interact with everyone and with God.

We are told God's requirements are to "act justly and to love mercy and to walk humbly with God" (Micah 6:8). In the wisdom literature of the Old Testament we are told to love God and keep His commandments (Ecclesiastes 12:13). Jesus states the greatest commandment is to love God with all your heart and with all your soul and with all your mind and love others as ourselves (Matthew 22:37–39). These actions are certainly a part of God's will for us. They set the framework for how we interact with God and how we interact with our fellow man. They are the basis for a civil society, and they are the basis for all our motives.

There are other scriptures which point to God's will for us. Paul tells us petitions, prayers, intercession, and thanksgiving should be made for all people, and we are to live peaceful and quiet lives in all godliness and holiness because this pleases God. Paul also states that God wants all people to be saved and to know the truth (1 Timothy 2:1–4).

The scripture tells us God wants our lives to be a living sacrifice, and we are not to conform to the thinking of the world; our thinking and our lives should be transformed by the renewing of our minds (Romans 12:1–2). God's word instructs us to give thanks in all circumstances because that pleases God and is his will (Psalms 69:30–31 & 1 Thessalonians 5:18). Peter instructs us to live for God according to the spirit (1 Peter 4:1–6). Peter also goes on to tell us to honor authority (1 Peter 2:13–14). These attributes are more than just things we are to know. All these attributes point strongly to things we are to do.

The heading for 1 Thessalonians 4:1–12 is "Living to Please God." This passage includes instruction about God's will, which is that we be sanctified, which means set apart. The items include avoiding sexual immorality. God calls us to be pure and live a holy life, and to love one another. We are told to make it our ambition to live a quiet life, to mind our own business, and to work with our hands so our daily lives will win the respect of others and we will not be dependent on anybody. These actions and avoidance of actions require commitment and obedience on our part. We can't just 'wish' our way into living a 'set apart' life.

In one of the passages from the Sermon on the Mount Jesus provides us tremendous insight into the will of God. Jesus said,

> *"You have heard that it was said, 'Love your neighbor and hate your enemy. But I tell you, love your enemies and pray for those who persecute you, that you may be children of your Father in heaven. He causes his sun to rise on the evil and the*

> *good, and sends rain on the righteous and the unrighteous. If you love those who love you, what reward will you get? Are not even the tax collectors doing that? And if you greet only your own people, what are you doing more than others? Do not even pagans do that? Be perfect, therefore, as your heavenly Father is perfect."* (Matthew 5:43–48)

The instructions Jesus provided were very specific. We are to love and pray for our enemies. There was no exception given.

Perhaps one of the most interesting short but powerful verses in scripture is this, "The world and its desires pass away, but whoever does the will of God lives forever" (1 John 2:17). This verse certainly implies that if our goals, our objectives, and our targets are focused on what this world says is important, then those rewards will be short lived and will not last. They will not make a difference in eternity. It is when we do the will of God that we 'live forever.'

It is important for us to realize we cannot earn God's love. His love is free and abundant. However, I believe we must realize God's will for us encompasses much more than the desire for us to make it into eternity with Jesus. God's will is made up of very intentional actions on our part which follow very specific instructions on His part. These actions require us to trust God for wisdom which only He can provide through the Holy Bible. We are not smart enough to substitute our mind for the wisdom of God. The actions also require obedience on our part. God's word is true, and we are told with certainty in Galatians 6:7 that we are not to be deceived, and God is not mocked, meaning I am not going to fool God; His word is true. I will reap what I sow.

When we consider all that God's word says, I believe our goals, objectives, and targets must be focused on loving God with all our being and about having our lives reflect Jesus in all our actions.

After sixty-seven years on this earth I realize more every day that Jesus cannot be reflected in my life or my actions by my own strength. While I do need to be knowledgeable about what the Bible says I should do, I have found knowledge is not enough. The Christian life—God's will—is about Godly wisdom being applied to our daily thoughts, motives and actions. When we focus on those things, we can count on the Holy Spirit of God to help us when we are weak.

When I read the Sermon on the Mount I realize that as much as I try to 'do everything' I still have my sin nature to deal with, and I must have the help of the Holy Spirit to provide correction, wisdom, guidance and empowerment. I have precious promises in scripture to help renew my mind, but if I am not focusing on my relationship with God daily, then I am not making use of the Godly knowledge He provides. I become like a rudderless ship drifting with the current.

One thing I have learned over the course of my life is there can be times when I have a legitimate question concerning how a particular course of action fits into 'God's will' for me or my family. These questions are what we might call gray areas. In my experience the gray areas could be about whether or not to accept an assignment in another city or perhaps where to worship. I have also had gray areas regarding where I should live. In these situations, the issue is not whether or not to follow the teachings of Jesus; the issue is knowing which course of action to take so I can maximize my efforts for God. Sometimes the decisions around those gray areas can be difficult to make. My wife and I sometimes joke about wishing God would write the answer in the sky for us. By the way, we have not had that happen yet. So, what do we do?

In Rod Handley's book, *Character Counts, Who's Counting Yours*, there is an excellent set of scriptures I have found to be very helpful when I have one of those gray area decisions to make. These scriptures provide guidelines which should be considered.

Guidelines For Gray Areas *

10 Key Questions To Ask

1. (Desire) Do I honestly desire to know God's will? (John 5:30; 7:17).
2. (Scripture) Is there a Scripture passage or Biblical principle to consider or apply?
   (Psalms 119:105; Mark 12:24).
3. (Prayer) Have I sincerely prayed and asked God what I should do? (Jeremiah 33:3; James 1:5; John 5:14–15).
4. (Counsel) What is the counsel of others, especially from those who know and love me and God's Word? (Proverbs 11:14; Proverbs 12:15; Proverbs 15:22; Proverbs 19:20).
5. (Loving others) Will doing this provide a loving example and build up others?
   (John 13:34–35; 1 Corinthians 8:9, 1 Corinthians 8:12; 1 Corinthians 10:24).
6. (Affect me) Will this help me to grow more like Christ, or could it potentially enslave me?
   (1 Corinthians 6:12; 1 Corinthians 10:23).
7. (Christ) What do I think Jesus would do about this? (1 John 2:5–6).
8. (Witness) Will doing this make me a more believable Christian and a better witness for Christ? (1 Corinthians 9:19–22; 1 Corinthians 10:32–33).
9. (Glorify) Will doing this bring greater glory to God? (1 Corinthians 10:31).
10. (Peace) Do I honestly have peace about doing this?
    (1 Corinthians 14:33; Philippians 4:7; Colossians 3:15)

*** Author unknown**

Rod Handley, Character Counts Who's Counting Yours (Handley, R. (1995). *Character Counts - Who's Counting Yours?* Grand Island, Nebraska 68803: Cross Training Publishing

When I use these questions to evaluate a situation, I have found the first thing I must do is be honest with myself and God. If I do not intend to be honest, then there is no point in trying to answer the questions, because I am really looking for a way to justify my desires and actions. When I am honest with myself and God it becomes easier to develop a sense for what the will of God is in my particular 'gray area'. If I start to feel a sense of guilt or concern with any of my answers to any of the ten questions, then there is a good probability the decision I am about to make does not line up with God's will for my life. If I can honestly sense the affirming of God's spirit in my heart after going through all ten questions, then the decision can cease to be a gray area from the standpoint of God's will.

After looking at the scriptures for guidance concerning what God's will is for us, I am convinced His will is much more than what we may have thought it to be in the past. I am also convinced we have the picture of God's will already revealed to us in His word, the Bible. We do not find any scriptures which indicate we should be focusing on the categories of our stuff, our position in society, our personal gratification, our entitlement, or 'our just because,' like we talked about earlier.

The scriptures, in fact, paint the picture of a true follower of Jesus as someone who wants to follow God's will and is focused on the realization that God loves them more than they can ever imagine. True followers of Jesus want to follow God's will out of a sense of thankfulness for God's grace and mercy and because they really do want to be obedient. The true follower is focused on loving God totally with all of his or her being and loving others as himself or herself. These actions are results of internalizing and living out the greatest commandment to love God with all our being.

When we make the decision to live our lives in that fashion, we can be assured we can know and follow the will of God (Matthew 22:37–39).

You see…, I do not believe the will of God is a secret. The question really becomes this, "When we know the will of God, what are we going to do with it?"

Thoughts to Consider

- How do I define will?
- Do I have an overriding goal for my life, one which supports all other goals?
- Do I consider God's commands to be part of His will for me?
- How does God's word define His will?
- What does being a 'living sacrifice' mean for us in today's world?
- Does God's will require intentional actions on my part?
- Can I live out God's will on my own strength?
- What do I currently do when I encounter a 'gray area' in my life?
- Is God's will a secret to me?

What Is the Abundant Life?

I want us to spend some time taking a closer look at what we see in John 10:10. The Bible tells us Jesus came so we could possess abundant life, so let's spend some time and effort digging deeper and learning what that means to each of us.

Current versions of the Bible render the phrase differently in the passage. The phrase used in the King James Version is, "life more abundantly." In the NIV the phrase is, "to the full." In the NASB the phrase is, "have it abundantly." The Message (MSG) says this, "real and eternal life, more and better life than they dreamed of." The New Living Translation (NLT) puts it this way, "a rich and satisfying life." The actual Greek word for abundant used in this passage of scripture is *perissos* (Strongs G053) which means the following: exceedingly, beyond measure, more, very highly.

When Jesus was talking with the Samaritan woman by the well at the village of Sychar we find her asking Jesus why He was speaking to her (John 4). After all, she was a Samaritan woman, Jesus was a Jew, and culturally this was a big deal which should not happen. In the conversation we find Jesus telling her some very interesting truths, the first being that if she only knew the gift God had for her and who it was who was speaking to her, she would be asking for more than water, she would be asking for living water. In Jesus's day the phrase living water was used to describe the presence or blessing of God. (Ourrabbijesus.com, Our Rabbi Jesus / His Jewish Life and Teaching, Insights from Lois Tverberg) Jesus goes on to describe water which will truly quench her thirst forever. The water would be a fresh, bubbling spring that is within and will give eternal life.

The picture painted here by the scripture is one of an extraordinary life. This is a life about much more than what people would consider normal. This is the kind of life that is about excitement—more than we can orchestrate ourselves. There is a sense of vibrancy as opposed to lethargy. This is a life which outlives our stay on this earth, this is eternal life. I believe this is what is being taught by the scripture when Jesus says we can have life to the full—we can have abundant life.

Let us take some time to briefly address what abundant life is not. The abundant life is not about the 'name it and claim it' gospel. If we define the abundant life as health, wealth, and prosperity, we run into some issues which are problematic when considering scripture. In 1 Corinthians 1:26–29 we are told few of us in the world's eyes will be powerful or wealthy. God chooses things which are powerless to shame the powerful. God chooses things that are despised and counted as nothing to bring to nothing the things the world finds important. The reality is no one can ever boast in the presence of God.

In Matthew 8 under the heading of "The Cost of Following Jesus" we see Jesus having an interchange with a teacher of the religious law. Jesus told the leader that even He did not have a place to lay his head. In Ecclesiastes 5:8–20 under the heading "The Futility of Wealth" the scripture writer makes it very clear by saying those who love money will never have enough. There is no doubt, we are not to aim for wealth. In fact, the Bible states an interesting truth which is often misquoted. Paul tells Timothy "the love of money is the root of all kinds of evil. And some people, craving money, have wandered from the true faith and pierced themselves with many sorrows" (1 Timothy 6:10). It is important to understand the issue Paul is highlighting here is the love of money, not money itself. The takeaway for us is to understand the love of anything other than God has the potential to yield something other than the abundant life.

When Jesus was being questioned by Pilate prior to going to the cross, Jesus clearly stated the Kingdom of Jesus was not of this world (John 18:36). We are provided with instructions about living a new life. The first thing we are to pursue is the realities of heaven. We are told to think about the things of heaven and not the things of earth. We are supposed to die to our old life and then have our real life be in Christ (Colossians 3). God's word is very clear. Our desires are to be for God and His kingdom. If our desires are not aligned with God's desires, then our desires will not help us live the abundant and full life Jesus came to give us.

I want us to look at the word 'blessed' as it is used by Jesus in Matthew 5:3–11, at the beginning of the Sermon on the Mount in Matthew 5-7. The Greek word used in the Beatitudes is 'makarious' (Strongs G3107). The word means more than just happy (Doctrine Matters, Bible Truths from www.BibleDebates.info, Does "Blessed" in The Beatitudes Just Mean "Happy").

One way the word has been described is that "our happiness is independent of our circumstances. It is self-contained, meaning that regardless of what is happening to us externally, we can be truly happy internally. We can be genuinely blessed as followers of Jesus Christ," (Christianity.com, What Does "Blessed" Mean, Greg Laurie, Taken from "Blessed" used by Harvest Ministries (used by permission).

William Barclay (The Gospel of Matthew, Volume1, Revised Edition, The Westminster Press, Philadelphia, Second printing, 1976) provides some valuable insight. Barclay says "blessedness which belongs to the Christian is not a blessedness which is postponed to some future glory; it is a blessedness which exists here and now. It is not something into which the Christian will enter; it is something into which he has entered. True, it will find its fullness and its consummation in the presence of God; but for all that it is a present reality to be enjoyed here and now." Barclay also says that "makarious then describes that joy which is serene, untouchable, and self-contained, that joy which is completely independent of all the chances and the changes of life." I believe these words provide us with an excellent picture of what an abundant life looks like.

I would suggest a key attribute or outcome of an abundant life is that we can be at peace regardless of the circumstances in which we find ourselves. I have observed this attribute in family and friends who have been in some extremely difficult situations. A dear friend of mine had cystic fibrosis, went through a lung transplant, and as a result of the disease eventually had her life cut short. I knew this person for more than twenty-five years and in all that time I never heard her complain. What I consistently saw and heard from her was thankfulness for the daily blessings of God. When we attended the memorial service for my friend, we celebrated a life well lived.

I remember a Sunday school teacher who had come from difficult circumstances. She was always there to help us kids know that God loved us and helped us grow up in His will. She showed her young students what it was like to live an abundant life. To this day I remember going into her classroom on Sunday evenings and hearing her tell us about the Bible characters. We knew by her actions she really did love us. There was a joy about her which was not caused by her physical surroundings; it was caused because she knew God loved her, and she really felt she was making a difference for God in the lives her young students. I would say she would definitely have described her life as blessed.

Let's examine the statements Jesus gave us regarding the attributes that bring about being blessed.

> 3 *"God blesses those who are poor and realize their need for him,*
> *for the Kingdom of Heaven is theirs.*
> *4 God blesses those who mourn,*
> *for they will be comforted.*

5 God blesses those who are humble,
for they will inherit the whole earth.
6 God blesses those who hunger and thirst for justice,
for they will be satisfied.
7 God blesses those who are merciful,
for they will be shown mercy.
8 God blesses those whose hearts are pure,
for they will see God.
9 God blesses those who work for peace,
for they will be called the children of God.
10 God blesses those who are persecuted for doing right,
for the Kingdom of Heaven is theirs.
11 God blesses you when people mock you and persecute you and lie about you and say all sorts of evil things against you because you are my followers.
12 Be happy about it! Be very glad! For a great reward awaits you in heaven. And remember, the ancient prophets were persecuted in the same way."
(Matthew 5:3–11 NLT)

In Barclay's commentary (p. 91-118) we find many insights regarding the Beatitudes. The first, (Matthew 5:3) being poor in spirit describes someone who knows he is totally helpless on his own, someone who has nothing at all. That person then realizes he must put his total trust in God, which frees him to become totally obedient to God; and he will become a citizen of God's kingdom. This is the picture of a man who has checked his pride at the door of life and knows he owes everything to God.

The second Beatitude (Matthew 5:4) is about those who mourn. The words here mean much more than just being sorry. Many times, we can be 'sorry' for our action or for a particular situation we are in. The word for mourn in this Beatitude is the strongest word used to connote mourning. It is the word used for mourning the death of a loved one. This is about having our heart broken for the suffering in the world and for our own sin. It is in this kind of sorrow that we realize what our sin caused Jesus Christ, the very Son of God to undergo on our behalf. We can then become joyful because we realize we are forgiven. We will be comforted.

Perhaps one of the most misunderstood of the Beatitudes is the third, (Matthew 5:5) the Beatitude about the meek. Sometimes we are tempted to believe it means we are to be in the background, we are to only speak when asked, we are just humble servants and we certainly do not want to be prideful. There are certainly elements of those attributes which are important such as humility verses a self-pride. We must always be on guard to make sure we are not putting ourselves first. We must always follow the leadings of God. However, the word used for meek (*praus*) (Strongs G4239) has a much richer meaning than the English word for meek conveys. Aristotle defined meekness (*praotes*) as the middle ground between *orgilotes*, which means excessive anger, and *arorgesia* which means excessive angerlessness.

There was also a second meaning for *praus* that had a standard Greek usage. It was the word for an animal trained to obey the command of its master. The animal (in this case a horse or perhaps an ox) was not weak; it was strong, yet under the total control of its handler. This Beatitude can then be translated: blessed is the man who is always angry at the right time and never angry at the wrong time! That man is totally under the control of God. He knows his own weakness. That man will be a leader.

The fourth Beatitude, (Matthew 5:6) blessed are those who hunger and thirst for righteousness, is an idea which is difficult for many of us in a modern western culture to relate to. We may be hungry and thirsty after participating in a sporting event or mowing the yard, or even playing with the grandkids, but we can get some water, a snack, maybe a PB&J sandwich and we are good to go for another round. We can wait for a real meal later in the day. Instead, this Beatitude is about being hungry and thirsty for the whole meal, all the food and all the water right now. In

Jesus's time people would have been better able to relate to this teaching because food and water were not as accessible as they are for us today. This Beatitude is about wanting all nourishment that is available, because the individual needs the food and water to survive.

Jesus tells us we should be desiring righteousness, meaning we want to do the right thing from God's perspective. A translation of this fourth Beatitude is that we will be blessed when we seek to do the thing God would have us do with as much intensity as a starving man longs for food and a man dying of thirst longs for water. This is about being 'all in' with God. The promise given in this teaching is we will be blessed and filled when we are hungering and thirsting with all our heart.

When we look at the fifth Beatitude (Matthew 5:7), being merciful, we might say to ourselves, "Oh that means to forgive someone; and I can do that, no problem." Later in the sixth chapter of Matthew we are told we must forgive to be forgiven (Matthew 6:15). There certainly is an element of forgiveness implied in this Beatitude, and we must start there. However, this is just the start of the meaning being discussed here. The Greek word used here for merciful is *eleemon* (Strongs G1655). The Greek word goes back to the original Hebrew and Aramaic word, *chesedh,* which means the ability to get inside another person's thoughts until we can see things through the other person's eyes. This is more than just pity; this is about making a deliberate effort to identify with the person. This is about being truly concerned about the person. This Beatitude could be translated to mean blessed is the man who inhabits the other person's being, sees with his eyes, and thinks and feels what he thinks and feels. When a person exhibits sincere caring behavior, he will find others will do the same thing for him. He will be shown mercy.

In the sixth Beatitude (Matthew 5:8), we find teaching about our motives. The word used for 'pure' is *katharos,* (Strongs G2513), and it has a variety of meanings. One of the meanings is clean, as in to wash clothes or to clean the chaff from the grain. *Katharos* was also used to describe the sorting of soldiers so that the discontented, cowardly, and unwilling were separated from the army and what remained were the true fighting men. It was often used with another Greek adjective to describe wine which had no water mixed in or metal which was pure and contained no alloy. One way to translate this teaching is blessed is the man whose motives are totally pure, not mixed with anything, because he will see God.

Now we will look at peacemakers, the seventh Beatitude (Matthew 5:9). The Greek word for peace is *Eirene,* and in Hebrew it is *shalom.* (Barclay's commentary (p. 108)). These words mean much more than the absence of trouble. If the absence of trouble were the sole meaning of peace, then we could say we are good if we wish to do no harm. This is a good place to start in our interactions with others but as is often the case, we are given a higher objective to attain. The Jewish Rabbis of the time loved to discuss the highest task to be performed, which was to establish a right relationship between men. Being a peacemaker is about being active in the process of reconciling people with each other. Jesus came to bring us into a right relationship with God. Is it any wonder we find in this passage of scripture that we will be blessed when we do our part to be actively involved in reconciling men to men? When we practice being a peacemaker, we will be called the children of God.

The eighth and ninth Beatitudes (Matthew 5:10–11) are ones we sometimes like to minimize. These teachings are about being persecuted and insulted. At first glance we can legitimately ask the question, "How can there be any blessing in being persecuted and insulted? What can those things possibly have to do with being happy?"

There are two attributes of the persecution and insults being discussed here which we must immediately examine. These attributes are key to the meaning of this Beatitude. The scripture is very clear; the persecution and insults we experience must be because of our pursuit of righteousness (doing right in God's eyes), and there must not be any truth to the accusations of which we are being accused. These are false accusations of evil. Jesus told his disciples they would have trouble in this world (John 16:33). They would not be able to stop those things from happening. Jesus told His servants they would not be above the master (John 10:24). We are to consider it joy when we face trials of many kinds (James 1:2–7). It should not surprise us when we are persecuted and insulted. Barclay makes the following observation about persecution. (p 118)

> *"It is inevitable because the Church, when it really is the Church, is bound to be the conscience of the nation and the conscience of society. Where there is good the Church must praise; where there is evil the Church must condemn—and inevitably men will try to silence the troublesome voice of conscience."*

You see, each follower of Jesus Christ is a part of God's church. It is inevitable that we will face persecution and be insulted. Those who have gone before us, the prophets and yes, even Jesus Christ himself suffered, and we are no different. It is our responsibility to make sure our actions are about righteousness. Then, when the persecution and insults happen, and they will, we are promised the kingdom of heaven. We can rejoice and be glad because we will have a great reward in heaven.

Let us examine one of the dynamics which relates to all the Beatitudes. It is important to note where Jesus was when He delivered the lesson and to whom He spoke. These teachings of Jesus were delivered from a mountain side. Jesus was not in 'church.' Jesus was talking to the crowds who were following Him. This was not a religious setting in any manner. In today's environment it would be somewhat like a large group of people sitting down in an outdoor field to listen to a local celebrity. Why is this important? I believe Jesus was telling everyone what they needed to do to be blessed. This implies that regardless of the background of the listener, it was possible to internalize the message and apply these teachings to their lives.

These teachings were not just for the religious leaders of the day—the teachers of the law. If the teachings were followed, they would bring blessedness to the listener regardless of his position in life. Sometimes we may be tempted to think that we want to be followers of Christ, but this 'fully devoted' thing is for the clergy, the teacher, the professor, or the really old 'saint.' We believe this blessed way of life is so beyond us we could never attain the level of maturity in our Christian walk even if we tried; so, we make the decision to bypass the effort all together. I believe this kind of thinking is a lie of the devil. The devil doesn't want us to be victorious; he wants us to doubt our relationship with God, become ineffective for God, and then eventually give up on the whole thing. God's word gives us a very different picture of what we are in Jesus when we are told we are more than conquerors (Romans 8). We need to step up and mature in our thinking. The blessed life is available for all who accept Jesus Christ as their savior and desire to live for Him.

We need to understand the Beatitudes are not an a la carte menu to choose from. The listeners were not given the option to choose whether to be solely poor in spirit, merciful, or a peacemaker, etc. They did not get the option to select their favorite Beatitude and exclude the others. This was also not a list to be prioritized. By their very nature, the Beatitudes are a package deal. Living the blessed life is meant to be an all-encompassing life. This concept is consistent with what we learn when we are told that if we stumble in one point of the law we are guilty of breaking it all (James 2:8–11). When we review the Bible, we are told to obey all the commandments, not just some of them. There is not a place in scripture where we get to choose what we want to obey and then ignore another instruction from God. Following Jesus Christ is an 'all in' deal. The same concept applies to the Beatitudes.

The last thing I want us to realize about the Beatitudes is that the list of Beatitudes does not include references to money, position, power, or any other physical attribute as being able to bring about the 'blessed' existence

Jesus is talking about. In fact, the list describes actions which have their basis in humility, mercy, integrity, peacemaking and righteous living. If we hope our stuff will bring about the state of being happy and having joy regardless of our circumstances, we are sadly mistaken. God's word is clear; we are to seek first the kingdom of God. It is in the process of seeking first the kingdom of God where we find true blessedness resides. This is where we find the abundant life Jesus came to give us.

I firmly believe the Beatitudes provide us with the very wisdom of God to show us what our responsibility is. After sixty-seven years on this earth, by observation and by personal experience, I believe with my whole heart it is possible to live the abundant life in Christ or Jesus would have not told us He came to give the abundant life to us.

I want to be very clear; I am not talking about perfection. God continues to show me where I have not made the best decisions, where I have failed Him and I will use the word 'sinned.' I can relate to Paul's words when he says what he wanted to do he didn't do and what he didn't want to do he did. He then proposes the following question, "Who will rescue me from this body that is subject to death?" He triumphantly answers himself with the following, "Thanks be to God, who delivers me through Jesus Christ our Lord!" (Romans 7).

I believe living the abundant life is about the process of becoming more like Christ as we go through our journey on this earth. All of us are in the process of maturing in our relationship with God. One of the individuals I consider to be a spiritual mentor would say, "We are a process and not a product."

When we first give our lives to Jesus Christ, we start the journey with Him as our Lord and Savior. Even though we are babes in Christ we are His, and God's love is lavishly given to us. However, there is a high probability we know very little about the significant teaching of God's word. We have started the process of becoming like Christ in our thoughts, motives, and actions. We are told to grow in the grace and knowledge of

Jesus (2 Peter 3). We are told we are like newborn infants, we are to long for pure spiritual milk so we may grow up into salvation (1 Peter 2). We are instructed to speak the truth in love and to grow up in every way like Christ (Ephesians 4). These scriptures tell us we are to be growing. Yes, we are to become like Christ, but the reality is we will still be maturing until our last breath.

All the individuals I have known who I would say have lived the abundant life would quickly say they have not achieved perfection. They are still in the process of becoming more like Christ. I believe Christian perfection is not a prerequisite for living the abundant life. However, I do believe seeking God first in our life is required to live the abundant life. We must be in the process of becoming what God would have us be.

We are provided a roadmap for becoming blessed and mature in Christ. The reality is through the certainty of the power of Christ in our lives we can be victorious (Colossians 1:25–28). We now have to do our part; it is time to invite Christ to be active in our everyday life. It is our responsibility to be obedient to the leading and empowering of God's Holy Spirit in our lives. It is time to move from a life of mediocrity and start the journey into the life Jesus came to provide for us, the blessed life, the abundant life.

Thoughts to Consider:

- How would I describe the abundant life?
- Are there things I love more than God?
- What does the word 'blessed' mean?
- Do I possess a genuine feeling of happiness in my daily life?
- How are the Beatitudes described by Jesus counter to today's culture?

- Is there a Beatitude I find hard to accept?
- Is the promise of the abundant life for everyone?
- What are the Beatitudes not about?
- Am I in the process of living the abundant life?
- Do I believe I can live the victorious abundant life?

God is Faithful, but We Make the Decisions

God is faithful in carrying out everything He has said in His word. We are reminded that because of the Lord's mercies we are not consumed, His compassions don't fail, they are new every morning, and the faithfulness of God is great (Lamentations 3:22–24). The Lord is ours, therefore we can put our hope in Him. We can rest assured God is for us. In Romans 8 we are given some of the most comforting words in scripture. We are told all things work together for good to those of us who love God, who are called to do His will. We are told nothing can separate us from God's love (Romans 8:28).

I have found these words to be true in my life and the lives of many people I have come to know and love. When I face trials beyond what I can control and imagine, God is there in the comforting presence of His Word; the prayers of people I do not even know and those who know me closely. There are acts of kindness that go beyond duty and spring from true Christ like love and are delivered with a timing only God can orchestrate with the only response we can make being to pay it forward.

I want to share an example with you. To me, this demonstrates the compassion which comes from God. My wife and I experienced this event after the birth of our third child. The background to this event follows.

Before we were ever married, we talked about how many children we wanted to have in our family, and we agreed that three would be a great number. We filed the talk away in our memory and proceeded to get married. After we had been married three years, we were blessed with our first child, a beautiful daughter. We were so thankful and proud. Twenty-one months later, after a picture perfect pregnancy, we were blessed with our second child, another beautiful daughter. Again, we were so thankful and proud. Our family was becoming complete. There were two diaper bags, two car seats, and some minor, well maybe not so minor sleep deprivation. Quite frankly, we were so busy we kind of forgot about the number three. We used the top of the piano to proudly display pictures of each of our children. Life was good.

One day I came home from work and Elaine (my wife) said, "Galen, there aren't enough pictures on the piano." To which I replied, "Well, let's go get some more pictures." Then followed Elaine's reply to me, "No Galen, there aren't enough pictures on the piano." It was at that moment where the discussion concerning how many children we would have came rushing back to my memory. After some discussion we decided to see if our family would expand. Elaine became pregnant and we were starting another chapter of our journey.

This pregnancy was not normal and there were some scary moments along the way. Elaine became extremely sick with HELLP syndrome. We were able to get excellent medical care. Elaine and our son Caleb came very close to dying. Caleb was born seven weeks early and weighed just two pounds twelve ounces. Elaine was in the hospital for a week before she was able to come home, and she was weak. We were thankful she and Caleb were doing fine. The outcome could have been vastly different. We were also disappointed we could not bring Caleb home yet. He was in the hospital for six weeks and weighed four pounds when we brought him home.

The evening Elaine came home from the hospital a man and wife from our church called and asked if they could bring some food. We said yes. When they arrived, they proceeded to bring in a feast. It seemed to us to be a heavenly banquet. When asked how we could thank them, their response was this, "Just pay it forward." At that moment two people walked out the door of our house who had just demonstrated the love and compassion of God to us. We ended up with another picture on the piano, and we are so thankful for God's provisions. I know everyone's story does not end up as great as ours, but I also know God is faithful to not leave us or forsake us. Regardless of our circumstances He sends people along our way to minister to us.

We are given a precious promise in Hebrews 13:5–6 which tells us to keep our lives free from the love of money, then we are informed that God has told us He will never leave us or let us be alone. We can say for sure the Lord is our helper, and we do not have to be afraid of anything man can do to us.

Since we know God is faithful, what does the rest of God's word say? I believe we need to be aware of the fact that at the end of the day we are the ones who make the final decisions about what we set as targets for our lives and what we do to hit those targets.

In Genesis two and three we see the account of the original fall of man. It should be noted that God's instructions were very clear, "But you must not eat from the tree of the knowledge of good and evil, for when you eat from it you will certainly die." (Genesis 2:17). So…what happened? Adam and Eve made the decision to disobey. It is vital to notice God did not stop them from making the decision and then eating the fruit. The responsibility for the outcome rested on them.

In Mark 8:34 we see Jesus talking to the crowd and His followers and telling all of them they must give up themselves and their desires and take up their cross if they want to follow Him. Jesus told them what was required of them. However, each person had to make the decision that day regarding whether they would follow Jesus. In Revelation 3:20 we have the words of Jesus saying He stands at the door and knocks. It is the responsibility of the person inside the room to open the door so Jesus can come in and dine with him.

A most interesting passage is where the believers are to let the Holy Spirit lead their every step because the things of their old selves are against the Holy Spirit (Galatians. 5:16–17). Their old self and the Holy Spirit are against each other so the believers are to avoid their own desires and let the Holy Spirit lead them. The believers had to make these decisions themselves; God's Holy Spirit would not make the decision for them. The Hebrew children were warned to not let their hearts become hard as their early fathers had done (2 Timothy 2:15). As believers in Christ, we are told to study and show ourselves approved unto God so we will not be ashamed, and we are told to rightly divide the word of truth (Hebrews 3:15). Christians are instructed to work out their salvation with fear and trembling (Philippians 2:12).

I believe the point is this. The Bible clearly says we are responsible for our decisions. God is all-knowing and therefore knows the best course of action for us in every situation. We can trust His leading. However, we are the ones who make our choices. Sometimes we get confused at this point and think we are talking about earning salvation, which cannot be done, this is not a salvation experience. We are talking about being obedient to what God's word says we need to do.

In the Old Testament we see a classic example of this. Samuel told King Saul to go and smite Amalek and utterly destroy all that Amalek had including men, women, children, and animals. Nothing was left off the table, everything was to be destroyed. When Saul went into battle, he spared Agag, the Amalek king, and the best of the sheep, oxen, etc. Not long afterward the word of the Lord came to Samuel concerning the disobedience of Saul. Samuel confronted Saul and Saul lied to Samuel and then Saul tried to pass the buck (1 Samuel 15). Samuel states one of the classic lessons we need to learn and the lesson is this; obedience is better than sacrifice (1 Samuel 15:22). In the New Testament we see Jesus state this same lesson. If we love Jesus we will keep his commands and we are told to have Jesus's commands and keep them. This is how we show Jesus our love for Him (John 14:15–21).

When we examined the Beatitudes earlier, we found there is an element of each of them for which we are responsible. We are the only ones who can take care of the pride issues in our lives. We have to understand what our sin has caused, and then we make the decisions to truly be repentant and mourn. Only we can decide to be obedient to God. We are the only ones who can decide to seek God's righteousness and then want the right things of God as much as we want food and water to live. No one except us can show mercy to someone who has wronged us. We are the ones who control our motives, and we are the ones who work toward peace in stressful situations. If we are persecuted and insulted because of our ungodly behavior, we will not be blessed. In each of these beatitudes we are participants and not just consumers.

We must be obedient to God's word, the teachings of Jesus, and the direction of the Holy Spirit of God in our lives. If we fail to act on what God has shown us, then we will miss out on the results which come from following God with our actions. It is our responsibility to allow God to direct us, and I believe this is a key to living an abundant life in Christ.

Thoughts to Consider:

- What does the faithfulness of God look like?

- Does God make my decisions for me?

- Who made the decision to disobey God in the beginning?

- How are obedience to God and our decision making related?

- Are there areas in my life where I have chosen to disobey God's command?
- How can I improve in my decision making process?
- Is there currently any area in my life where I know what to do but do not want to make the decision to move forward?

Settng Goals, More Than Wishful Thinking

Sometimes there can be a tendency in Christianity for followers of Christ to view the process of setting goals and the planning of what we need to do or of what we need to become as a sign of not trusting God. This belief says we should trust God for everything, which is true. We are told to trust God with all our heart and to not lean on our own understanding (Proverbs 3:5–6). Some will point to God's word stating that without faith we cannot please God. Those individuals then will say the setting of goals and planning shows a lack of faith.

God's word is abundantly clear; we must have faith in God because it is faith which motivates us to action. However, we need to carefully view the rest of Hebrews 11:6 which states we must believe God exists and He rewards those who earnestly or whole-heartedly seek Him (Hebrews 11:6–7). This a picture of more than just waiting on God; this is about seeking what God would have us do. God has promised to guide us, to give us the plan. We then need to be obedient and execute the plan we have been given. You see, Noah believed God existed, and he believed God cared about him. The faith which Noah had led him to prepare for the flood. Noah did not wait for a big boat to show up on the scene. Noah followed the plans God gave him and Noah built the ark. He acted on what he knew to do.

The apostle Paul talks about pressing on toward the goal to win the prize (Philippians 3:13–14). This scripture presents the image of an athlete who knows what they want to accomplish. The athlete is willing to go through the training and pain to accomplish the goal. This is not a picture of sitting around and waiting for God to intervene. The same theme is carried through where we are instructed to run in the way required to win the prize, to go into strict training and to not run as someone who runs aimlessly (1 Corinthians 9:24–27). In Proverbs we are told to put our outdoor work in order and have our fields ready before we build our house (Proverbs 24:27). This scripture paints the picture of us prioritizing our responsibilities and taking care of the most important things first. It is critical for us to consider the ways of the ant and be wise (Proverbs 6:6). Ants are always working toward a goal; they do not sit around and wait to be fed. All these scriptures help show us we are to be actively involved in our lives. If we choose to go through life without actively setting and pursuing goals we are described as being sluggards, unwise and running aimlessly.

In Matthew chapters five, six and seven we have what is commonly referred to as the Sermon on the Mount. In these chapters Jesus provides the basic set of instructions for us to follow in life. The topics Jesus speaks to include the following:

- how to be blessed
- how to be viewed by the world
- righteous living
- interaction with our fellow man
- lust and adultery
- divorce
- oaths
- vengeance

- loving enemies
- giving to others
- prayer
- fasting
- what we treasure
- worry
- petitioning God
- discernment

At the end of the teaching Jesus provide us with an interesting comparison. He tells us about the foolish man and the wise man. Both men heard the instructions and both men faced the same set of issues: the rain came, the streams rose, and the winds blew against the house. The foolish man is said to have built his house on the sand. Jesus described the foolish man as a person who heard the words of Jesus and decided not to put them into practice. The result for the foolish man was that his house fell with a great crash. Jesus described the wise man as a person who built his house on the rock; someone who heard the words of Jesus and put those words into practice. The result for the wise man was very different from the result for the foolish man; the house of the wise man stood firm (Matthew 7:24–27).

The Biblical concepts Jesus gave the crowd that day show us we are to work diligently toward fulfilling the teaching of God's word. We need to aim at the correct set of goals and then we need to daily put into practice the steps necessary to accomplish those goals. Both the Old and New Testament provide us with the picture of the overriding concepts by which our behaviors are evaluated.

First let's look at the overriding concepts about the goals which are given in the Old Testament. In Exodus chapter twenty we find the Ten Commandments being given to Moses and the Hebrew children:

- have no other gods before God
- do not worship idols
- do not take God's name in vain
- honor the Sabbath
- honor our parents
- do not murder
- do not commit adultery
- do not steal
- do not give false witness
- do not covet

These commandments provide the basic set of expectations by which all behaviors were to be measured. We are instructed to, "act justly and to love mercy and to walk humbly with God" (Micah 6:8). These words provide guidance for all our motives.

In the New Testament we see Jesus having an interchange with the Pharisees (rigid followers of the Old Testament law). The Pharisees wanted to trap Jesus and have Him make a statement, which went against the teachings of the Pharisees. Jesus lays out what is commonly referred to as The Great Commandment. Jesus replied:

> *"Love the Lord your God with all your heart and with all your soul and with all your mind. This is the first and greatest commandment." And the second is like it: "Love your neighbor as yourself."* (Matthew 22:34–37)

These words of Jesus provide the framework in which all our thoughts, motives and actions must fit. If we are motivated to have a goal which cannot be supported by these commandments, then we need to reevaluate that goal and allow God to help our thinking mature.

In the second chapter of James we are provided with the contrast of faith and deeds. Faith would say we must trust in God, which is totally true. This scripture also supports the idea of faith and works going hand in hand. This passage says even the demons believe there is one God. It goes on to say Abraham was considered righteous for what he did as he offered his son Isaac on the sacrificial altar.

Here is a brief recap of Abraham having faith in God and then obeying God (Genesis 22). God told Abraham to go to the land of Moriah and sacrifice Isaac; Abraham obeyed. It is important to note Abraham followed the plan as God had set it in motion. Abraham did not question God, but he took the necessary items to make the journey. He was following God's plan. He took the wood and the fire. He listened to God and went to the right place. He built an altar for the sacrifice, and he had the knife. Abraham bound up Isaac and laid Isaac on the altar. All the while Abraham was trusting God to provide the sacrifice. Abraham had the plan and executed the plan to the best of his ability. Abraham had to go through all the steps required to sacrifice his son. At the last second God was faithful and God provided the sacrifice. Abraham's trust of God and his action of obedient faith worked together, and it was the working together which made the faith of Abraham complete. For Abraham, having faith in God was more than just wishful thinking, it required action.

The Bible is very clear, saying when we accept Christ as our Savior, we become a new creation, "Therefore, if anyone is in Christ, the new creation has come: The old has gone, the new is here:" (2 Corinthians 5:17). Since we are a new creation, we are called to have a new set of goals for our life and we are to actively pursue those goals. Some of our old goals and targets could have been to make more money with our personal pleasure being our highest priority. We may have wanted to be 'the man' everyone respected. Those goals are based solely on what we can get from this world and are all about us. When we become new in Christ, we have an opportunity to replace those old goals with new goals which are focused on God and others. We can allow our new goals to change our behavior and make a difference in the lives of others for eternity.

One of the great truths of God's word is Jesus telling us He will not leave us or forsake us (Hebrews 13:5). Jesus promises as we love Him and keep His commandments, He will ask God to send us the spirit of truth, the Holy Spirit, to be with us and live in us. Jesus tells us He will not leave us as orphans but will come to us (John 14:15–18). As we start and continue the process of aligning our goals with the heart of God, we can be sure we will not be left alone. God, through the presence of His word, and the empowering of the Holy Spirit, can help us as we desire to become more like Christ. I believe it is in this process of becoming like Christ where we learn to more fully experience the abundant life which Jesus talked about. These new goals are more than wishful thinking, they become part of the process of renewing our minds and redirecting our thoughts, motives, and actions.

Thoughts to Consider:

- What is the relationship between setting goals and trusting God?
- What does my 'taking action' have to do with trusting God?
- What are the overriding concepts upon which I set my goals?
- Am I asking God to help me develop the goals for my life?
- When faced with a decision, do I move forward when I know the direction to go, or do I wait for more information?

So, What are Our Personal Goals Anyway?

I have found it is vital for me to have a set of personal objectives that serve as overriding principles to help guide my daily actions. Without those overriding principles I find it easy to slide back into ways of thinking and habits. Sometimes, after the fact, I have to step back and analyze my actions against my objectives and determine why I made a particular decision, evaluating whether the result was what I really wanted. Paul talks about the tension between what he knows is wrong and right and what he really does (Romans 7). There is nothing magic about having personal objectives in themselves; they do not make me do anything, but I have found they help me keep the things I really want to accomplish, the targets I want to hit, in the forefront of my mind.

Another dynamic of my personal goals is that I am responsible for the thoughts and behaviors I am wanting to accomplish. Having a set of personal goals or targets is about taking ownership for my own actions. I will be impacted by people and circumstances, both past and present, but I cannot use those influences as excuses for my behavior. I am the one who makes the final decision to act the way I do.

One of the important things to consider is how to make objectives. There is a tendency to set incredibly lofty goals or ones that are so vague we can't really define what success looks like. We then set out with the best of intentions only to become discouraged when we are not sure we are making progress. An example of this is to have a goal of being more Christlike. While this is in fact the overriding desire of my heart it is also so lofty it becomes difficult to articulate what I am going to do today to work toward accomplishing the goal. When I do fall short of an expectation or feel I have missed what God would have me do, I can start to feel defeated. When this happens the devil is quick to tell me what I am wanting to do is impossible, so why try?

Another example of a goal which is not well defined and becomes vague, is the goal to lose weight. This happens to be a goal I have had multiple times in my life, and I have found every pound I have lost. The problem with this goal is it that it doesn't define for me what the final weight should be, how long I am going to take to get there, and most importantly the behaviors I will need to adopt daily to hit the target.

I have found I need to have structure to my objectives. To provide structure I use the concept of SMART objectives. For the last several decades the concept of SMART objectives has been used in business management. The November 1981 issue of *Management Review* contained a paper by George T. Doran titled *There's a S.M.A.R.T. way to write management goals and objectives.* The paper discussed the importance of objectives and the difficulty of setting them.

***SMART** goals and objectives have the following attributes:*

- Specific—a specific area for improvement
- Measurable—quantify or at least suggest an indicator of progress
- Assignable—specify who will do it
- Realistic/Relevant—state what results can realistically be achieved given available resources
- Time-related/Time bound—specify when the result(s) can be achieved.

The advantage of SMART goals is having something I can define and then develop specific actions I will commit to. These actions help me get past the emotion of having a lofty desire and get to the action steps required for me to accomplish a task, improve a situation, change an attitude, or become more like Christ. These actions move me from faith without actions to faith and actions working together, which is discussed in the second chapter of James.

We need to understand things change in life, and we need to adapt to our new situation.

It is important to note there are seasons in life. In the third chapter of Ecclesiastes we are given a picture of the different stages in life which most of us will find ourselves going through. I am now retired after a career of forty-six years with a company. Our children have left home and we now have sons-in-law, a daughter-in-law, and grandchildren, not to mention some grand pets. My body does not work quite the same way it did when I was nineteen. I realize time marches on, and I have limited days on this earth to make a difference for God. These dynamics of my life need to be taken into account and the appropriate set of goals developed to fit the time. Some of my personal goals do not change (man after God's heart) while some (good employee) need to be revisited.

I believe my relationship with God is the most important relationship I have. All my actions and everything which happens in my other relationships is impacted by my devotion to God. Because of this personal belief, my first objective or target is to be a man after God's heart. I have made a commitment with myself and with God to have the following targets I shoot for:

1. Daily time in prayer with God.
2. Daily time in God's word.
3. Regular worship attendance.

The behaviors required to hit these targets could include the specific amount of time in prayer and God's word. However, I choose to leave room for some flexibility but still have something which is very attainable. I also did not describe a specific location because I am sometimes away from home due to business travel and vacations. I wanted the target to be something which could be accomplished regardless of the time zone or the physical location. I found these targets to be realistic.

My second objective is about the most important relationship I have on earth which is with my spouse. Elaine is the child of God who He has sent to be my companion as I walk on this earth. This is the most intimate earthly relationship I have and it deserves nothing less than my total love and commitment. There are attitudes and actions I must take on to help my spouse know she is loved by me and by God. It is an awesome privilege and responsibility, and in many ways should mirror my relationship with God.

To be a Godly husband, I commit to the following:

- Daily communication with my spouse.
- Daily affirmation of my spouse.
- Have a weekly date with my spouse.
- Have a biannual getaway with my spouse.

There are some assumptions built into these behaviors, primarily that daily communication be loving, respectful, and honoring. Because I try to have those attributes be part of our marital conversation, I did not include them in the target but there would be nothing wrong with including them. One thing I did not try to define was a 'date.' I wanted to have Elaine help as she desires. The same concept applies to what the biannual get away looks like. Going to my favorite skeet range does not a 'date' nor 'getaway' make.

My next objective is about the second most important relationship I have on earth and this is with my children. I am to love them unconditionally, to teach them by my actions; and if I must by my words. I have the responsibility of showing them what a Godly father looks like, for it is in those interactions between me and them where they learn to trust their Heavenly Father. I have the responsibility of showing them what a Godly man looks like. With God's help this can be a very fulfilling endeavor as I watch them mature and watch them make their faith in God their own.

My third target is to be a godly parent, and to do this I commit to the following:

- Daily communication with my children.
- Daily affirmation of my children.

This was easier to do when the children were still living under our roof because I had the opportunity to see each child daily so the objective worked. Now as we are 'empty nesters' I am needing to look at the target and make some significant adjustments. The children and their families live in three different states, have different schedules, and are at different points in their lives. One family has two children and both spouses work outside the home. One family has three children with one of the parents being a stay-at-home mom. One family is happily enjoying their first year of marriage. While I will need to adjust the frequency of the communication, I have control over the frequency, and I can certainly be affirming in all communication.

Following the objectives concerning my most significant personal relationships is one about the physical body God has given me. I understand I am a steward of that body. In 1 Peter 4:10 we are told we should use whatever gift we have received to serve others because we are to be faithful stewards of God's grace. We are not able to efficiently carry out this responsibility if we totally disregard the body which God has given us.

This is not to say we can't help others know God as we go through physical issues in our lives. Often, through those difficult times we are able to witness to others about the peace and power only God provides. Some of the most influential Christians I have known have had to deal with serious health issues, and through those times they have challenged me to grow in my faith. However, we do have a responsibility to do our part to maintain healthy bodies and minds. Instead of being able to contribute to God's kingdom by using my gifts in an active way, my health can become a problem which sometimes has a very detrimental impact on my ability to fulfill my responsibilities to my family and to God. There are things I can do (diet, exercise, and sleep) which can help my body be more effective.

The fourth target is to have a healthy body, so I commit to the following:

- Exercise 45 minutes five days a week
- Eat correctly
- Get at least 7.5 hours of sleep per night

I have not tried to define the exercise. Sometimes I bicycle, walk, workout on an exercise machine, and on rare occasions swim. I have found with a little creativity I can make something work. I realize exercising seven days a week is not realistic, however there are very few times I can't exercise five days a week. Eating correctly implies amount and type of food. I have an app on my smart phone I use to track calories against a target. Sleep is a matter of discipline for me and when I fail, I don't reset the time commitment, I reset my behavior.

My final objective is about my interactions where I work or volunteer. While I have listed this objective last it does not mean I feel its importance is diminished. It is in those interactions with others I often sow the seeds for how others see God. In many ways my interactions outside my immediate family can help people be hungry for God or cause those people to not want to have anything to do with God. We need to understand this is serious. We have a responsibility to be kind, compassionate, effective workers modeling integrity in all we do.

We are instructed to do everything with all our hearts as if God is our master and we are working for Him (Colossians 3:23). As a follower of Christ, I want those around me to see someone who does their part or more, performs quality work, and someone who is willing to be part of the solution to issues that arise.

The fifth target is to be a good employee, volunteer, neighbor, so I:

- Work as for the Lord
- Do everything with integrity
- Choose my words and actions carefully

Although I am retired, I still use this target for any volunteer activities I pursue. I want people to see my behavior and ask why I do what I do. This then gives me an opportunity to tell others what God has done for me. I have found this goal serves me well in retirement. In retirement it can be easy to shift gears from being engaged in life to going into neutral. What I am learning is there are still things to accomplish, and just because I have retired from a vocation, God has not taken away the abilities He has given me. The need to serve God has not gone away. Part of doing everything with integrity is being a good steward of what God has provided.

In the Old Testament we see the account of Caleb, one of the original twelve people Moses sent to go into Canaan to spy out the Promised Land. The Hebrew children disobeyed God and did not immediately go into the Promised Land. Approximately forty-five years later we find Caleb addressing the Hebrew children by informing them that even though he is now eighty-five years old, he is still as strong as when Moses sent him out forty-five years earlier. He gives all the credit to God for keeping him alive while Israel moved about in the wilderness (Joshua 14). There are at least two things at work here; Moses said Caleb would have an inheritance in Canaan, and Caleb did not 'retire'. Caleb remained true to the Lord and God honored Caleb's dedication.

All my goals, targets, and objectives work in concert to help me be more in tune with what God really values. They help me have a clearer understanding of my responsibilities and what I need to do to meet those responsibilities. All this starts with me getting in touch with who God is. He is my creator, Jesus is my savior, and the Holy Spirit has been promised to be my helper. I have no excuse for failing to step up to the plate and becoming engaged in God's will for me and how He wants to use me in His kingdom.

One key to being effective in God's kingdom is making sure my targets are aligned with the Word of God. All my personal targets have provided me with overriding principles I strive to follow each day. They provide a picture of what I need to think and do on a daily basis. A most interesting dynamic about targets in my life is that without them I tend to react to the situation without a well thought out plan and the result can be something I am not proud to own. What we choose to aim at will impact the rest of our lives. I pray all followers of Christ will understand what God's goals are for their lives and then be dedicated to hitting those targets.

Thoughts to consider:

- What guides my actions?
- Do I always take ownership for my actions?
- Are my goals so lofty they are hard to define?
- Are my goals so generic success can't be defined?
- What season of life I am currently in?
- Are my goals appropriate for my season in life?
- Am I doing everything as if I am doing it for Christ?
- Am I retiring from what God would have me do?

It's Time to Set Some Goals / Targets

We have looked at several things up to this point, including the idea that the battle starts in our minds. We must first focus on God, because only He can provide the wisdom we need to live life abundantly. We have examined the concept of living an abundant life as opposed to a mediocre life. We have looked at what God's word teaches us about setting goals. If we have no goals we become like a rudderless ship driven by the wind and waves.

We have looked at attributes of effective goals and how those attributes translate into actions which can be purposeful and impact our lives. We examined some of my personal goals as an example for us to think about. We have looked at what God's word says about His will for our lives. We have discussed the fact that God is faithful, but it is each of us who make the final decision as to what we choose to do in every situation.

All these things lead us to the next step in the process. That step is to develop individual goals / targets for our lives. This process can be a little scary. When we start the process it is easy to feel we are about to make commitments we may not be able to live up to. None of us likes to fail, and we now have something to be accountable to. What will happen if we fail? We will discuss that question a little later because it is a question with which virtually all of us wrestle.

Another question which comes up is how many of these targets can we realistically incorporate into our lives? Will we be able to focus on multiple things and succeed at all of them? Will we be disciplined enough to work toward the successful completion of the goals/targets?

Our personal targets should not be focused on items which are temporal in nature; where the outcome has a definite / defined ending and is about material stuff. Examples of those kinds of targets could include earning 'x' amount of money by the time we retire. They are not focused on working or living in a particular location. Our personal targets are not focused on what level we will rise to in our employment. They are not focused on the correct number of children for our family or which schools we or our children should attend. It is important to note there is nothing inherently wrong with these items because in each of them God can direct our thoughts and have the results glorify him if we follow where His Spirit leads. These things make up some of the elements of our lives and God is interested in us having an abundant life. They are, however, not things which impact our character, the renewing of our mind. Our goals should help our core being become more like Christ; and our mind begin to think like Christ would think.

Anything we experience in life impacts the extent to which our life is abundant. Peter gives us the following instruction, "Cast all your anxiety on him because he cares for you." (1 Peter 5:7). This scripture is a favorite for many Christians and provides us with the wonderful promise that as we humble ourselves under God's hand, He will lift us up in due time. We can bring all our anxieties to Him. We are told to rejoice in the Lord always, be gentle, not be anxious for anything, and in all things to pray and to ask God with thanksgiving. Then God will provide Christ's peace which is beyond our understanding and peace which can protect our minds (Philippians 4:6–7). When we cast our anxieties on Jesus, humble ourselves before God, and rejoice in the Lord, we are freed up to allow the peace of Christ to protect our minds.

Paul tells us the Holy Spirit is here to help us. The Holy Spirit prays through us and for us. He knows us and helps us be in God's presence. Because of this we can be assured God can work in every situation of our lives for good (Romans 8:26–28). God cares about the daily things which make up our lives. We are certainly following His instruction for us when we bring these things to Him. We can trust in His word.

It is not my desire to state what the personal goals for other Christ followers should be. The process for determining those goals is something between each individual believer and God. Each of us has areas in our lives where God has gifted us and areas where we can make progress from our current state. I believe that determining our targets should be a matter of fervent prayer. Seeking wisdom from God's word is a great place to start. I have found I need to be honest with myself and honest and humble with God. If we have unforgiven sin in our lives we need to heed the words of King David in Psalms 32:1–5:

> *"Blessed is the one whose transgressions are forgiven, whose sins are covered. Blessed is the one whose sin the Lord does not count against them and in whose spirit is not deceit. When I kept silent, my bones wasted away through my groaning all day long. For day and night your hand was heavy on me; my strength was sapped as in the heat of summer. Then I acknowledged my sin to you and did not cover up my iniquity. I said, "I will confess my transgressions to the Lord." And you forgave the guilt of my sin."*

In the Sermon on the Mount Jesus tells us if a worshiper was coming to the altar to offer a sacrifice and then he remembered he had wronged another person he must first go back to the person and make the situation right before he came again to offer sacrifice (Matthew 5:23–24). This was an illustration which would have been clear to the audience Jesus was speaking to that day. The idea of sacrifice was simple. If the man did a wrong thing between him and God, the sacrifice was what was required to restore the relationship. The Jews of the day understood the relationship between man and God could not be made right until the relationship between man and man had been made right. (William Barclay, The Gospel Of Mathew, Westminster Press, Philadelphia. Pennsylvania, 1976, p.142)

These scriptures indicate it is vital for us to take care of unfinished business with God and man if we want to grow to maturity in Christ. It is important for us to sincerely and reverently approach God with nothing being hidden between us and our fellow man. If we want God to direct the targets of our lives, we must first be honest and repent of our sin.

It may be helpful to seek wise counsel from someone you have great confidence in and you trust. Paul told the Ephesians that Christ gave them the apostles, prophets, evangelists, pastors and teachers to equip Christs followers (the church) so the body of Christ might be built up, move in unity, and become mature followers of Christ (Ephesians 4:10–14). It is not a sign of weakness, but of strength, to seek wise counsel. Solomon tells the young people to “let the wise listen and add to their learning and to let the discerning get guidance for understanding proverbs and parables, the sayings and riddles of the wise.” (Proverbs 1:1–6). Fearing God (honoring Him as our creator and Lord) is the beginning of knowledge but the fool despises wisdom and instruction (Proverbs 1:7). If we are serious about setting the direction of our life we must acknowledge God and not be afraid to ask for wisdom.

When I was employed, I tried to adhere to the following conceptual format when developing objectives:

1. State each objective as a phrase and not a complete sentence full of business jargon. This allowed me to be able to memorize all the objectives and tell them to others very quickly.

2. Limit the number of objectives to no more than six. Again, this enabled me to commit them to memory. It also helped me keep focused on what was critical. If the critical doesn't get done the non-critical stuff is just that, non-critical, and I fail.
3. Limit the number of key activities to no more than four per objective. I found I could commit the key activities to memory.
4. Each key activity had to be an activity where I was totally responsible for the outcome. I did not allow myself the option of passing the buck. I owned the result. Therefore, there could be no shared objectives
5. Write down my objectives in my planner so I always had them for reference. Objectives in a three-ring binder on a shelf can soon become forgotten.

This objective / target setting process forced me to look at what was most critical to the mission I was attempting to accomplish. I was forced to take responsibility for my actions. I found this same conceptual format served me well in the setting of my personal objectives.

You may have heard the story about the steel mill that cut a huge hole in the side of the building. The mill was sold to new owners, and the new planet manager was taking a tour of the plant for which he was now responsible. When he saw the huge set of aircraft doors in the side of the building, he asked the production manager (PM) why the doors were there. The PM explained the production line was critical to the output of the whole plant. There was a very large piece of equipment which must be swapped out as quickly as possible when it failed to operate because the plant would lose hundreds of thousands of dollars every hour the line was down. The doors allowed for moving the whole piece of equipment out of the line and a new piece of equipment moved in and installed in record time. The new plant manager complimented the plant staff on their ingenuity.

The new plant manager looked at the situation a few minutes and then asked what caused the equipment to fail. The communication happened as follows; PM, "The shaft starts getting hot, the machine stops, and the drive train locks up. New plant manager, "Why is it getting hot?" PM's response, "It is a big shaft." New plant manager, "Why is it getting hot?" PM, "Can't get enough air to cool it." New plant manager, "Why is it getting hot?" PM, "must be a design which didn't take into account the way we operate." The new plant manager went to the shaft in question and noticed a valve with a quarter inch line which went to a bearing housing deep inside the drive train. The new plant manager asked, "What is that valve for?" PM, "We don't know. We didn't know it was there." The new plant manager then opened the valve, oil started flowing and the shaft became cool.

The concept of the story we just read is this: We need to be careful when we start to look at things we want to address, and make sure we are going to make a change in something which will address the real issue. In the case of the steel mill the issue was not about the original design of the equipment. It was not about how the equipment was to be operated or even how quickly the machine could be changed. The real issue was about lubricating the bearing which had been designed into the original machine from the very start. For some reason, no one knew the purpose of the valve and it had been totally forgotten by all the personnel at the plant. They were focused on the short-term goal of getting the product out the door for the next hour, day, week, etc.

It is easy for us to get sidetracked by the details of our everyday activity. We have work to do. We have kids to get to school. There are groceries to buy and meals to prepare. There are doctor appointments to go to. We have the house to clean, cars to maintain, and stuff to do. These things demand our time and we want to do a good job. We must get the product out the door. Everything seems to run according to plan, at least until there is the breakdown; the car needs a significant repair, someone in the family gets sick, a job situation has a drastic change, or we get the call from school about an issue. What do we do then? Do we open up the big door on the side of our plant and put in a new machine or do we do the hard work of seeing what actually went wrong and how we can eliminate it from happening again? Yes, we must take care of some things immediately, but we don't want to miss the opportunity to allow God to provide us with new wisdom and guidance. We might find we have a target which needs to be adjusted.

In our time on earth the real issues of life we face, such as feeling close to God, managing money, mending and developing strong relationships with others, feeling wanted, having an abundant life, etc. may require us to examine our lives with honesty and determine what is really impacting our thinking and behavior. We may need to have the new Plant Manager help us evaluate the situation, provide us with His wisdom and then put in place the changes which can truly make the situation improve.

I believe my primary target needs to be how I can incorporate the wisdom and will of God into my mind. This personal target then sets about changing my thoughts and actions as I walk through life on this earth. That is why I choose putting God and learning His ways for me as my overarching target. My belief is that it is out of the process of continuing to grow in my relationship with Him from which everything else flows.

The second set of targets are about me fulfilling my responsibility to love others as myself. These guide my actions to become more 'others centered' and help me show God's love to all the people with whom I come in contact.

As you go through the process of determining the set of targets for your life, I would offer the following suggestions:

- Be honest with yourself; seek out what is really happening in your life.
- Spend time with God: go outside, get alone with God and allow Him to speak to you through His creation. As the psalmist said many times we need to 'be still' and know that He is God.

- Spend time reading the word of God. The Sermon on the Mount might be a good place to start. Every year I make sure I read Matthew 5, 6, and 7, and the books of James and Proverbs. I have found they provide incredible wisdom from God.
- Seek out wise counsel and allow that person to bring a more mature perspective into your life.
- Keep the main thing the main thing. Do not become overwhelmed with big changes with issues which might only require just a small tweak.

Remember, when you develop your set of targets you are not making a static set of things to do. You are making a dynamic road map for how to get where God wants you to go. You are developing a new way of thinking. It is important to understand what you develop can be changed and should be changed as situations change.

My belief is that all my targets must fit under the greatest commandments we are given by Jesus, which are to love God totally and love others as ourselves. There is nothing greater than these commandments. Loving God totally keeps our relationship with Him fresh and new. The command to love others as we love ourselves helps keep those relationships alive and up to date. Notice the command to love others doesn't say we aren't to love ourselves. After all, we are created in the image of God, and He loves us supremely. We are fearfully and wonderfully made. We are so valuable Jesus died so we could have a relationship with God. It is extremely important for us to understand we are all created by God with the same love and passion for our well-being. What we are told to do is love others just like we love ourselves. These two commandments provide us with a good place for us to align our objectives.

As we go through our journey on earth we grow, we mature, our circumstances change, and we need to allow God to help us to continually be in the process of becoming more like Him. We must allow our minds, our motives, and our actions to become more like Christ. The goals and the targets we shoot for can become life changing. As we put in place new ways of thinking, new targets, and as we work toward those targets, we truly do become the new creation Paul talked about (2 Corinthians 5:17) as we journey down the road of an abundant life.

I pray God will guide all of us as we allow Him to shape our thinking through the establishment of goals and targets for our lives. God is faithful, and He has promised to walk with us as we pursue becoming more like Jesus.

Thoughts to Consider:

- Is my life like a rudderless ship?
- Are there elements of setting personal goals that scare me? If so, what are they?
- Will I allow God's word to shape my core goals?
- Am I willing to be honest with myself and with God?
- Am I willing to commit to seeking God's wisdom for me?
- Do I have unfinished business with God and/or people?
- Am I committed to using the objective setting process?
- Are my objectives focused on the 'main thing'?
- What do I let keep me from focusing on the main things?
- Am I listening to the new Plant Manager?

What To Do Before We Pull The Trigger

Once we have developed a set of targets which will help us be engaged in the process of becoming more like Christ, we are ready to embark on a great journey with God. We will be challenged and rewarded as we move forward. Sometimes we will experience multiple emotions as we travel this journey. We may feel joy for the progress we are making in an area of our life. We might experience concern or sadness because we feel our progress in other areas of our lives is going slower than we would desire. It is possible to have these emotions all at the same time. Perhaps this will be one of the greatest journeys of our lives as we develop into what God would have us become.

In 2018 I had the pleasure of retiring from a company after spending over forty-six years working in various positions. Since that day I have had the opportunity to spend more time with kids, grandkids, and friends. I have also been able to become more active in photography, a hobby I have dabbled in for over forty years. I have also had the opportunity to start a new hobby, shooting trap and skeet.

The dynamics of the game of skeet are quite interesting. On average, the clay pigeons / targets (referred to as birds and made of clay formed into a disc) travel at approximately fifty-five miles per hour. The birds have a diameter of 4.252 inches. The average shot at the bird is around twenty-two to twenty-five yards with some shots much closer and some shots farther away. The speed of the projectiles (bbs in the shotgun shell) might be between 1,000 feet per second (FPS) to 1,200 FPS. Add into the mix there are many variations of shotgun types which can be used (over/under, pump, semi-auto), variations of shotgun gauges (410, 28, 20, 16, 12), and variations of shotgun ammunition which can be used. There are various sizes of projectiles (bbs) in the shotgun shell and the speed of the bbs will vary. To shoot a 'round' of skeet the participant shoots from seven different positions (called stations) around a semi-circle and one station at the center of the semi-circle. On some stations the shooter shoots a double. A double is when two birds fly at the same time from opposite directions and the shooter attempts to break both birds, one immediately after the other. There are many things to manage at the same time. The game could be a metaphor for life; many things to manage at the same time.

I was first exposed to the sport at a public shooting range. There were guys like me who had never attempted to shoot skeet before and then there were 'the regulars.' We have all seen these guys, whether it be fishing, archery, bowling, golf, trap, skeet, target shooting, or the Christian walk. We have the blessing of being around those individuals who by their performance exhibit the ability to hit the target. They are often more senior individuals who have stories to tell. In skeet shooting, they have the ability to walk up to a shooting station and smoothly call for the bird by saying, "pull", or some other very personalized facsimile of pull, and then seemingly without aiming, the shotgun goes boom and the bird is hit. Sometimes the bird turns to powder (the ultimate hit). The shooter then, often without much emotion, proceeds to the next shot. They make it look so easy that everyone tends to say the same thing, "I can do that."

When I found myself on the skeet range and starting to take my first shots at the clay pigeons, I quickly realized that while I was somewhat competent with using a camera to capture an image or using a firearm to hit a stationary target, I had no natural talent with the shotgun to hit a moving clay pigeon on the skeet field. It was much harder than it looked. I was tempted to tell myself there was just no way I could manage all the variables and be successful.

I found myself needing to go back to the basics of what I needed to do to hit the targets, in this case to break the birds. I knew what I wanted to the outcome to be. I wanted to have the clay pigeons break into many pieces; the more the better. However, having at least two pieces being created from what was once one small flying clay disc would work.

When I think about what I want to be as a Christ follower, a godly husband, a godly father, a good employee/volunteer and have a healthy body, I realize there is more to the attaining of the outcome than meets the eye. There are times I wonder if I can control all the variables and be successful. What am I to do?

There are those who have been on the journey longer than I have and/or have had different life experiences than I have had. They can make being a Christ follower look easy. They seem to be naturals. When I talk with those individuals I have found they all share a common trait. None of them automatically arrived at their current level of ability. They have all made a habit of asking for God's help in their lives and then obeying the direction they received from Him.

Even though they are now more mature in their walk with God they continue to ask for God's wisdom and then make the personal choices required to obey what God's word sets forth regarding how they are to live the Christ follower life. They each admit they are in the process of becoming more like Christ. I have never met one of those individuals who tell me they have arrived at what God would have for them. They all say they continue to be in the process of becoming more like Jesus Christ.

Let's evaluate some of the steps which are required to hit the target, whether it be a stationary target 'the bull's eye', the flying clay pigeon, or living the life Christ came to provide for us. That life is an abundant life, a full life (John 10:10) and a life of peace (John 14:27) which can't be attained in any way other than following Christ.

Regardless of the discipline I am wanting to improve on or the target I am wanting to hit, I have found the following steps enable me to have much greater success than trying to figure it out on my own. The steps I use to hit the target include the following:

- Don't be pridefull / Get help from the 'the regular' guy
- Identify the target
- Identify the weapon
- Pay attention to the fundamentals
- Eliminate distractions
- Focus on the target
- Execute
- Analyze the results
- Practice
- Don't give up

Let's evaluate the process of using these steps in our Christian walk.

Don't Be A Know It All, Find the regular guy

I have put finding the regular guy as the first step in hitting the target because I realize there is so much more to know about anything than I currently know. When I try to learn a new skill, or start a new habit it is important for me to understand when I try this on my own strength and knowledge I am exhibiting a tremendous amount of pride. When I think I can do it on my own, somehow, I decide I would not benefit from the learning of others. I let my pride start to control me. In Proverbs 16:18 we are given the following wisdom, "pride goes before destruction, a haughty spirit before a fall." This scripture paints a picture of failure for us if we allow pride to control us. The wisdom of God lets us know God hates pride and arrogance (Proverbs 8:13). Another wisdom passage states that fools are consumed by their own lips, and their words progress from folly to wicked madness (Ecclesiastes. 10: 12–13). The problem is when I follow the mindset that says I know more than the expert; I have to reinvent the wheel all over again. I fail to learn from the failures and successes of those who have gone before me.

Wisdom says a wise man will become even wiser when he receives instructions. He will increase in learning (Proverbs 1:5). We need to sit down and count the cost to see if we have enough money to complete the task of building a tower (Luke 14:28). The heading for Proverbs 8 is titled *Wisdom's Call*. This chapter discusses understanding, gaining prudence, wisdom more precious than silver, gold and rubies, etc. (Proverbs 8). All these teachings from God's word, the very mind of God, tell us we need to avoid pride and look to God, our creator, for the answers to our questions and the direction for our life.

So…the first thing I did when I started the process of learning to shoot skeet was to watch all the shooters who were on the hill (what we have affectionately renamed the shotgun range) and see who was successful. While I had tremendous sympathy for those of us who had zero to very limited experience in the sport, I chose to spend my time getting to know the people who demonstrated they knew what they were doing. One of the first things I learned from those individuals was while equipment was important, it was not the most important thing. The most important piece of equipment was what sat in between my ears.

We can look in God's word and see many examples of individuals who had what we might call a mentor/mentee relationship. From the 17th chapter of Exodus through the 24th chapter of Joshua we see the story of Joshua. Moses worked with Joshua and Joshua became a military leader, one of the twelve spies sent into the Promised Land. Joshua and Caleb were the only two individuals from the previous generation of fighting men who were allowed to enter the Promised Land. It was Joshua who led the Hebrew children into the Promised Land. We can only guess at the influence Moses had on Joshua. In 1st Kings 19 through 2nd Kings 2 we find the story of Elijah and Elisha who walked together serving God. There is no doubt Elisha was influenced by what he experienced with Elijah.

In the Gospels we see Jesus calling the twelve disciples to follow Him. For approximately three and a half years Jesus walked with these men and taught them about who God was, who He was, as the Son of God, and why He must die on the cross. The world is still being impacted by those men. In the book of Acts we see accounts of the Apostle Paul working alongside several early church men and women. These individuals included Silas, Barnabas, Timothy, Lois, Eunice, Phoebe, Priscilla, and Lydia to name a few. What we can learn from these accounts in the Old and New Testament is we are not meant to go through this life alone. We all need fellowship, which comes from having a relationship with our 'regular guy', our mentor.

I have a mentor, a gentleman who is almost twenty years my senior. He has been through all the stages of life which I have been through plus one generation. He has been a Christ follower for more years than I have been on the planet. He will be the first to say he is not perfect, but he will also speak to the faithfulness of God in his life. He helps me with perspective as I go through life. My life is much richer because of him speaking into my life. I have found the 'regular guy' in him. Oh, by the way, he also is a bird hunter.

So… as you start your process of hitting the targets God has for you, do not fall into the trap of thinking you can manage on your own the variables which exist to live up to what God requires. Do not neglect your 'regular guy'. Pray specifically for that person in your life and my belief is God will provide. This can become the first step in hitting the target.

Identify The Target

The next thing we need to do is to define at a personal level what the targets are for each of us. This is where we take the objectives we developed earlier and then focus on the key activities which go with each of our objectives. These key activities become the behaviors we focus on performing. In effect they become the immediate target.

Let's look at an interesting interchange between Jesus, His disciples, and the crowd as they were on their way to the villages around Caesarea Philippi. Jesus asked the group who people were saying Jesus was. The disciples replied some people were saying He was John the Baptist, others were saying Jesus was in fact Elijah, and others were saying Jesus was one of the prophets. Jesus asked the next question, "But what about you?" "Who do you say that I am?" To this question Peter replied Jesus was in fact the Messiah (Matthew 16:13–20 & Mark 8:27–30). I believe the concept to be learned here is Jesus wanted His disciples to have a personal relationship with Him. He wanted them to own what they knew about Him. Just going along with the crowd was not going to work. They were identifying themselves as part of His immediate followers.

Sometimes we have a tendency to identify ourselves, and by default, the things we are trying to accomplish with a particular group of people. As an example, I am blessed with a Christian heritage which goes back three generations on my mother's side of the family tree. My great-grandparents were very devout followers of Christ. My maternal grandfather was a pastor at one time. He and my grandmother started a church. My mother has been a Christ follower nearly all her life. At the time of this writing my mother is eighty-nine and continues to be a strong influence for Christ in my life.

It would be easy for me to look at my family history and say, "I want to follow in the footsteps of my family; that is what God would have me do." This certainly is a worthy way of life to pursue. However, I need my own relationship with God. I believe this requires me to personally seek

God and His direction for my everyday walk with Him. The accounts of my ancestor's lives with God can certainly be inspiring, but I need to take responsibility for my walk with God.

We can read about strategies for improvement and use the information gained to shape our habits. We can talk to others and have them tell us how they address a particular facet of accomplishing the task at hand. In today's world we can access the internet and get more data than we can possibly sort out. We can see videos from the experts and sometimes videos from the so-called experts. We can talk with our regular guy and gain the perspective of someone who has walked the road before us. There can be value in these sources of information, but at the end of the day it is God who made us and knows us the best. He can show us what we need to have in focus.

Perhaps one of the clearest examples of what our targets need to be can be found in Paul's letter to the Ephesians. In this passage we find a very comprehensive list of behaviors which come under the heading of *Instructions for Christian Living.* The instructions include the following do's and do not's: do not live like the gentiles, do not have hard hearts, do not live sensual lives, do not be greedy, do not give the devil a foothold, do not steal but do useful things instead, do not let any unwholesome talk come out of our mouths, do not grieve the Holy Spirit.

In this same passage we are told what to do: put off the old self, make a new attitude in our minds, put on a new self which is created to be like God in true righteousness and holiness, put off falsehood and speak truthfully, when we are angry do not sin, build up others, get rid of all bitterness rage-anger-slander-and every form of malice, be kind and compassionate, and forgive each other (Ephesians 4:17–32).

We need to evaluate our current behaviors in view of the scriptures and allow God to speak to us. When we are sincerely wanting to find God, He has promised to reveal Himself to us (Jeremiah 29:13). However, we are to ask with more than a casual curiosity. We must be asking because we really want to know what God, our creator, wants to tell us. God has promised

He will answer us when we call (Psalms 38:15, Psalms 20:6). King David said God will instruct us, teach us, and counsel us with his loving eye on us (Psalms 32: 8–11). So, as we walk through the steps of identifying our personal targets let's ask for the Holy Spirit of God to direct our hearts and minds. He is our creator and friend and wants the best for us.

Identify The Weapon

When I go to the range I have several choices to make. One of those choices is to decide which weapon I am going to bring. The choice I make is totally determined by what I am wanting to accomplish—by the target which am I trying to hit. If I am trying to keep all my shots within a two-inch group at twenty-five yards I might choose to bring my youth model single shot twenty-two caliber rifle with open sights. I still have the gun my father gave to me when I was eleven years old. It was a great gun for learning the skills required for shooting. The action was simple. The gun only holds one bullet, and the firing pin has to be manually cocked before the gun will fire. The gun is short so it fit my body and I could grip it well. Most everything I shot at with the gun was within twenty-five yards so the open sights worked well.

If I am trying to keep all my shots within a one-inch group at one hundred yards I will bring a different weapon. The bullet will be traveling faster, and the sighting system will not be open sights. I will add a scope so I can more accurately see what I am shooting. If I am going to be shooting at a clay pigeon I will be using a shotgun. This gun shoots a shell with several very small bbs (sometimes up to 461 bb's at one time), and the gun has no sights. I just look down the top of the barrel.

The point is I need to understand what I am trying to accomplish so I can bring the correct equipment and have the best chance for success. When I talk about the spiritual weapons I use it is vital I understand these weapons are designed to change the way I think, to get my mind and heart aligned with God. They are not designed to help me do something to another individual.

As an example, I may need to really seek God's wisdom concerning where He would have me attend church and where and how He would have me be involved in the local church body. This specific target will require me to spend time in God's word, to research a particular church body, and to listen to the direction of the Holy Spirit. I need God's direction to help me understand what is causing the questions in my mind and spirit. The time required to make this kind of decision may be longer than shorter. There may not be an immediate need to make a decision. The overriding weapon I need to seek is Godly wisdom, and then I need to act on what I learn.

On the other hand, the situation may be one where the Bible is clear. For example, if there is an issue between myself and a fellow believer, then the weapon I must use is to be obedient to what I already know God's word provides as specific direction in my situation. I must seek God's wisdom to guide my actions toward my spiritual brother. While there is always an element of God's timing, we must be careful to not hide behind 'waiting for the right time' as opposed to obeying God's instruction.

Let's examine one of the best descriptions about who and what we are really fighting against and the elements of which our weapons are comprised. The first thing to realize is our struggle is not with other people. Paul's analysis is clear, "our struggle is not against flesh and blood." If we see someone, a particular person, as the enemy, the target we are aiming at, then we need to reevaluate our understanding of the situation. Paul is clear on the identity of the enemy.

Paul describes the enemy as the devil's schemes. He then goes on to mention rulers, authorities, the powers of this dark world and the spiritual forces for evil. In the first part of John 10:10 we are told the thief (meaning the devil) comes only to steal and kill and destroy. In John 8:44 Jesus described the devil as a murderer from the beginning and the father of lies. It is important to understand the devil does not want us to succeed in hitting the target, in becoming more like Christ (Ephesians 6).

In the same chapter Paul goes on to describe the full armor of God. Paul uses the armor of the Roman soldier to illustrate what we need to use to stand against the schemes of the devil. In a very real sense these pieces of armor become our weapons, how we can hit the target of becoming like Christ.

We are to have the belt of truth. This means God's truth is what we lean on to counter the lies of the devil. God's word tells us the truth will set us free (John 8:32). We do not have to be sucked in by the lies of the devil.

Next comes the breastplate of righteousness, which means we do what is right in the eyes of God. Jesus tells us if we hunger and thirst for righteousness we will be filled (Matthew 5:6). We have the promise of Jesus Christ which says righteousness will not be withheld from us when we seek it as if our life depended on it. The breastplate protects our vital organs from harm. If we leave those organs unprotected the results can be catastrophic. When we seek to do the things which are right in God's eyes our heart and soul will be protected.

We are then told to be ready to show others the gospel of peace. This readiness acts like our shoes. Shoes enable us to walk and run over terrain without causing us to slow down or take different routes. They help us go over obstacles in our path. I remember as a young boy my family lived in the country in mid-Missouri. In the summertime we would often go to the Niangua River to go swimming. The surroundings were picturesque and the water was very cool. Sometimes we would walk along the riverbank looking for rocks, arrowheads, and other cool stuff. I still remember what it was like to navigate the rocks with no shoes. I could eventually get where I wanted to go, but the process was slow and often I had to take detours. With a pair of shoes the journey was quick and direct. When we set out to hit our targets we need to be equipped with the shoes God gives or the journey will be slow and tedious.

We are to add the shield of faith which will put out the flaming arrows the devil launches at us. We are told we can't please God unless we have faith (Hebrews 11:6). The reality is I have never seen God face to face nor have I seen any of the men of the Bible. I have to accept by faith that God exists and loves me. Faith in God keeps us shielded by His power (1 Peter 1:5). If I don't have faith to accept God's power and act on the power He provides, then I will just sit and hope something good happens.

We are told to take the helmet of salvation, which means we are to focus on what Christ has done for us on the cross. The reality is we can't protect our minds by focusing on what 'we' are trying to do to become more like Christ. We must always remember what Jesus did on the cross to bring us into a relationship with God. We can then rely on God's spirit to continue to make our minds new.

We are told to use the sword of the Spirit which is the word of God. We must use scripture to stand against the devil and allow the very Spirit of God to direct our thoughts and actions.

Paul tells us to pray in the spirit with all kinds of prayers and requests. Paul goes on to say we are to be alert and always keep praying.

These things make up our armor. They provide the ability for us to be victorious in our life journey. They are the tools we have at our disposal, the weapons we use to hit the target.

Pay Attention To The Fundamentals

I have discussed things I always consider prior to shooting at the target. One is to consider everything my mentor, my teacher has taught me about how to be successful. The next is to define exactly what I want to accomplish. Is the result the two inch group at twenty-five yards or am I wanting to turn the clay bird which is traveling at fifty-five mph into powder? I then make sure I have brought the weapon which will give me the best chance for success.

Once I get to the range I always go through a checklist every time I step into the shooting station and I get ready to pull the trigger. I pay attention to the fundamentals required for safety regardless of what I am going to shoot. Whether I am shooting with my bow, my handgun, my short-range rifle, my longer range rifle or my shotgun, I always go through the same checklist, made up of the following components:

- Always keep your firearm pointed in a safe direction.
- Treat all firearms as if they are loaded.
- Keep your trigger finger outside the guard and off the trigger until you are ready to fire.
- Be certain of your target, your line of fire, and what lies beyond your target.
- Always wear appropriate eye and ear protection when shooting and maintaining your firearm.

It is important for me to realize I am getting ready to take an action which I cannot take back. Once the trigger is pulled, the projectile will not return to the gun; it will go somewhere, and there will be consequences. If I have followed the concepts spelled out by the fundamentals, I will be able to hit closer to the target and not hit something I do not want to hit. As a shooter I must understand the serious nature of what I am doing. As a range instructor I must watch very carefully to make sure all shooters on the range follow the fundamental precautions. It is vital for everyone's safety.

We need to evaluate some of the fundamental concepts regarding our Christian actions and behaviors as we strive to hit the targets we are aiming at in our Christian walk. I believe the following scriptures provide valuable insight into what some of those fundamental concepts are; the things we need to consider as we focus on the targets we have set out to accomplish.

Jesus told his disciples about the vine, its branches, and bearing fruit (John 15:1–5). Jesus begins this teaching by saying every branch of the vine is to bear fruit. This is the fundamental reason the branches exist. The branches are not attached to the vine just to look pretty or provide some shade. In fact, if the branches do not bear fruit, those branches will be cut from the vine. If a branch does bear fruit it will be pruned so it can bear more fruit. Jesus also states being connected to the vine is vital because we cannot bear fruit if we do not remain connected to the vine. We are told we will bear much fruit if we remain attached to the vine. This concept becomes fundamental to our success for God.

Paul provides insight into the fruit of the spirit: Love, Joy, Peace, Patience, Kindness, Goodness, Faithfulness, Gentleness, Self-control (Galatians 5:22–23). The results of our actions should in some way produce the fruit Paul referenced. When we look at the list of fruit we can say with conviction that we want our actions, and our lives to produce this fruit. We can see the fruit of the spirit should be a fundamental list by which we examine the results. There is no argument concerning that point.

An interesting dynamic of all the fruit of the spirit is each one is only fruit as we live the fruit out in relationship with another person and/or our relationship with God. The fruit is not something to be set on a shelf or in a display case; the fruit is comprised of attributes we exhibit with others. If we are setting targets for ourselves which are all about how good we are going to look, we need to re-evaluate our targets and make sure they line up with what God's words sets forth.

I have found value in examining another list. This list contains fruit in stark contrast to the set of fruit from the list we are given by Paul. The list reads like this: hate, worry, strife, agitation, unkindness, dishonor, treachery, harshness, and instability. If the results of our actions are producing the second set of fruit, we can be assured the fruit is not from the Spirit of God. This fruit ultimately comes from our own desires. This fruit comes from our own envy and selfish ambition. We are told these things do not come from heaven but instead come from this earth and are unspiritual and demonic (James 3:13–18).

So, when we examine the two contrasting sets of fruit I believe we can say the fruit of the Spirit should be a fundamental set of dynamics we use to evaluate our actions. Before we pull the trigger or initiate actions we need to honestly evaluate those actions and with God's help, try as best we can to determine what will be the fruit of those actions.

Peter tells us Jesus provides divine power in our lives so we can live a Godly life. He provides promises so we can escape the evil desires around us and instead share in the divine nature of God (2 Peter 1:5–8). The scripture tells us because of the power and promises of Jesus, we are to make every effort to add to our faith, goodness, and then knowledge, and then self-control, and next perseverance, and next mutual affection, and finally love, with each building on the preceding quality. At the end of this passage Peter makes an interesting statement; Peter tells us if we possess those qualities in increasing measure, they will keep us from being ineffective and unproductive in our knowledge of Jesus Christ. The implication here is that without those qualities we will not produce fruit.

We are told to trust in the Lord with all our hearts and lean not on our own understanding. We are to acknowledge God in all our ways, to submit to his instruction and then He will make our paths straight (Proverbs 3:5–6). The reality is if we want our paths to be straight we must submit to the instruction of God. There are times we are tempted to try to hit our targets based on what we believe to be true. It could be we are sure we are right. We don't want to change. It could be we know there might be a better way to accomplish what we want but it will require us to change our current behavior which would be a lot of work. So, we do the same thing over again; we don't want to change. The instruction given in Proverbs is clear; if we want our path to be straight, to become easier to accomplish, there is no other way than to submit to God's instruction.

Our plans will fail when we have a lack of counsel; when we try to perform in our own wisdom and strength (Proverbs 15:22). When we have many advisers, our plans will succeed. We need to listen to advice and accept discipline because in the end we will be counted with the wise (Proverbs 19:20–21). We can have many plans but in the end what prevails is the purposes of the Lord. The fundamental concept here is we need wise counsel to succeed. We can't do it on our own.

One day on the range I had the opportunity to shoot with a very good skeet shooter who had been shooting shotguns for more than twenty years. My shooting experience that day was a very humbling one, as I would pull the trigger only to see the clay bird fly unimpeded away from me as I missed but yet another shot. The gentlemen turned to me after a series of less than spectacular shots by me and indicated the mechanics of how I was holding the shotgun looked good. He then asked me, "What are you aiming at?" I thought the answer was simple so I said, "the bird." To which he replied, "I know, but what are you aiming at?" I then replied, "What do you I mean?" He then replied, "You need to be aiming at where the bird is going to be, not where the bird is." We discussed the concept, and I had a decision to make. Oh, by the way, did I mention he was a very experienced shooter of more than twenty years and a skeet/trap shooting instructor? Was I going to ignore his advice or was I going to listen and try my best to do what he said? I chose to listen and do what he said. So on my next shot I tried to the best of my ability to put into practice what he told me to do. The result has been consistently improved scores since that day.

At one point in my career I was given the responsibility to deliver some information to a set of employees concerning the future of a work group in our part of the company. The information would force some employees to make decisions regarding their future with the company. I had done the research concerning the options available to those employees. I practiced how I was going to deliver the information. The meeting would not be easy. I really did care about the future of each individual. I spent time in prayer asking for wisdom and trying to understand how the information would be received by the impacted individuals. The day came to deliver the information, and I felt ready for the meeting. I delivered the information to the best of my ability. Under the circumstances the meeting went well. Follow up actions were initiated and we were moving forward.

I had prepared for the situation and then executed the plan. I followed the script, and it worked. I felt like I had done a good job. I was back in my office when the phone rang. An individual from another work group in our part of the company asked if I had time to talk, and I said yes. For the next few minutes, I was informed of real concerns about my ability to think clearly and make good decisions. I listened as best as I could. I had not prepared for this phone call from another part of the organization. I felt like I had to respond. So, respond I did. I did not call anyone names or use foul language. After all, I was a Christian and I was taught I shouldn't use foul language. I did, however, in no uncertain terms explain the fact I didn't appreciate the call and let the caller know they were ill-informed and needed to change their perspective. Then I hung up the phone knowing in my mind everything I had said was true. I pulled the trigger.

As soon as I placed the receiver back on the phone I realized I had just made a serious mistake. You see, there were many things I could have and should have done better. Some of those things would include immediately praying silently for God's wisdom, focusing on the questions and concerns and not about my hurt pride. After I heard the concerns, I could have said I needed some time to respond in a more comprehensive manner. The fact is there was nothing which dictated to me to respond immediately, but I did respond; I pulled the trigger and I could not pull the words back. As a result of my behavior I got to explain the situation to management. I sought out the individual and we had a face-to-face meeting where I apologized for my behavior.

I spent time in prayer with God asking His forgiveness. I knew I had not been a good representative for Him. I had taken my eye off the target, which was to be a good representative for the love of Christ. The fruit of my actions was not patience, kindness, goodness, gentleness, and self-control. Instead, the fruit looked more like the other list: strife, agitation, unkindness, dishonor, harshness, and instability. I had responsibility for choosing which fruit I was going to produce that day, and I made the wrong choice. When we don't pay attention to the fundamentals we do so at our own peril.

The point is, there exist some fundamental concepts and principles laid down in God's word which should be so familiar to us that they guide our thoughts. We are to apply those principles to our attitudes and actions as we move forward in our daily walk with God. We must understand we are to produce fruit, and we must remain connected to the teaching of Jesus and the power of the Holy Spirit. The fruit we are promised help in producing is all about our relationships with God and others. We must follow the instruction of our Heavenly Father and not trust ourselves. We must have wise counsel and put into practice what we are taught. When we do those things, we can be confident we are doing the fundamental things required for hitting our targets.

Thoughts to Consider:

- What are the variables in my life which must be managed?
- Am I in the process of becoming more like Christ?
- What steps do I need to take to enable me to hit the target?
- Do I have a regular guy, a mentor?
- Do I have a pride problem?
- Have I identified my personal target?
- Am I using the right weapons in my life?
- What do I consider to be the enemy of my soul?
- What can I do to use the armor God provides?
- What things do I consider being fundamental to my Christian walk?

Let's Get In The Game and Pull The Trigger

Let's imagine we are now at our position on the range. We have found our regular guy, identified our personal target, we have the correct weapon in hand, and we are practicing the fundamentals. We believe we are now ready to shoot, so what do we do next? We have the knowledge, it looks so easy, anybody can do this, and we are ready. It is now time for us to concentrate and perform. Concentration is made up of three elements and is where everything we have learned comes together. We must eliminate distractions, focus on the target, and then pull the trigger.

Over the course of my life, I have experienced my tendency to do what I have always done. It seems so easy and natural. I have learned responses and I let those guide my thoughts and actions. The problem comes when I am wanting to experience different results from those I have experienced in the past. When I fall back into following the same patterns of behavior I have always used, I find my results mirror the past and do not bring about the change I desire. If I fail to concentrate, I will continue to use whatever habits and behaviors I have programmed into my brain in the past. The results of my efforts will not change unless I change my actions. I must apply the new knowledge to my thinking and turn those learnings into action.

Concentrate: Eliminate the Distractions

Let's examine the first element of concentration; eliminate the distractions. Distractions come in many forms. I may be tempted to be held hostage by the past. I need to understand the past is just that, the past. I must eliminate distractions. When I am on the range with other shooters it can be tempting to wonder what they think of my performance. Do they think I am doing things right? Do I have the right equipment? Do I fit into 'the club'? Am I making any progress at all? All these things can start to come into my mind and I start to think more about "what they…" (you fill in the blank), think than what I am going to do next. One of my regular guys continues to tell me I need to block out everyone else who is on the range. When my turn to shoot comes up I need to mentally see myself as the only person on the range. This is my time to do what I do; the past and the impressions of others simply do not matter.

Each of us is tempted to look back at our lives. We have all had experiences where we felt our efforts were incredibly successful and probably there were times when we felt like we blew it. These events/times in our lives are part of our individual walk through our lives on this earth. The good thing is we can learn from those experiences. The problem comes when we let those events control our future actions. If we allow ourselves to be held hostage by past experiences, those experiences become distractions and hinder our ability to move forward.

We know that all of us have sinned and fallen short of God's glory (Romans 3:23). If we claim to be without sin, we deceive ourselves. On the other hand, if we confess our sin God is faithful and just and will forgive our sin and purify us from all unrighteousness (1 John 1:7–9). These scriptures point to the fact we all have a past. They also give the promise that God is faithful to forgive us and purify us. We can't let our pasts distract us from the promises of God in the future.

The apostle Paul talks about not having confidence in the flesh. Paul described himself as a 'Hebrew of the Hebrew', a Pharisee, zealous in persecuting the church, and based on the law, his righteousness was faultless (Philippians 3:5–6). In the eyes of his fellow Pharisees Paul was 'the man.' His past could definitely be a distraction compared to his experience on the Damascus road (Acts 9). So, what was he to do with the past? Paul declares this one thing he will do, forget what is behind and strain/reach for what is ahead. He was going to press on toward the goal of winning the prize for which God called him in Christ Jesus (Philippians 3:7–14). Paul made the decision to not be distracted by the past but to look to the future.

Paul tells us to put aside the deeds of darkness and put on the armor of light (Romans 13:12). He also instructs us to put off our old self (Ephesians 4:22), and we are told to throw off everything which hinders us and the sin that so easily entangles us (Hebrews 12:1). All these scriptures illustrate that we must not be distracted by the past. We are to move forward. In my case it does me no good to focus on the past times when I didn't shoot the score I wanted. I must eliminate those distractions from my thinking.

Focus On The Target

The second element of concentration is to focus on the target. When shooting skeet or trap the current teaching is the shooter is to visualize hitting the target, get into the correct stance, hold the shotgun correctly, soft focus on a particular area, call for the bird, and then focus on the bird as the bird comes into peripheral vision. From the time the bird is released our focus is not to leave the bird. When shooting stationary targets the shooter is told to get in a comfortable stance, control his breathing, and then focus the sighting system on the target. In each discipline focus on the target is essential.

Matt Emmons was an American finalist in the fifty-meter three-position rifle competition in the 2004 Summer Olympics. Matt had reached the finals and seemed like a lock to win a second gold medal. Emmons had a commanding lead over the other competitors and really only needed to get close to the dime sized bull's eye to win. He had won this competition before. "When I shot the shot," said Emmons, "everything felt fine." However, the shot did not show up. Matt had aimed and hit the target in the next lane over. The mistake gave the gold to Julia Zhanbo of China and Matt came in at eighth place. (Shayne Lopper, Hitting the bull's eye—on the wrong target, https://Brookline.wickedlocal.com/article/20120108/NEWS/30108997).

Matt was one of the elite shooters in the world, and yet he made a serious mistake. The reality is that he failed to aim at the correct target. Everything else was perfect, equipment and execution. He did hit a bull's eye, just on the wrong target.

One of the teachings Jesus Christ provided for us is found in Matthew 6:25–33. In this passage we see Jesus addressing the topic of worry. He tells us to not worry about what we eat or drink, about our body or about what we wear. Jesus instructs us to look at the birds. They do not sow, reap, or store away in barns but God feeds them. Jesus continues by telling us to look at the flowers. The flowers do not prepare their clothes but their appearance was superior to what the richest/wisest man on earth was able to accomplish. Jesus says God even clothes the grass of the field which is temporary. Jesus then tells us not to worry about these things.

At the end of the passage Jesus provides instruction about what we are to seek in our lives. He tells us to seek the kingdom of God and the righteousness of God. He then says we should not seek the things God will provide such as food and clothing and goes on to tell us not to worry about tomorrow. Christianity.com (Christianity.com, What is the Kingdom of God? Understanding Its Meaning) states when we seek the kingdom of God, we are asking for the rule and reign of the kingdom of God in our lives. We are under the lordship of God, and He is in control of our lives. They go on to state this kingdom is not about rules and regulations, but it is about "righteousness and peace and joy in the Holy Spirit" (Romans14:17).

As Christians, focusing on the target implies our desires are secondary to what God desires for us. We are brought back to what Jesus Christ stated as the greatest commandment for us. (Matthew 22:37) Jesus replied, "Love the Lord your God with all your heart and with all your soul and with all your mind." Regardless of what we would like to have our focus be, there is no doubt; we are to focus on putting God above all else with our whole being.

Pull The Trigger

The third element of concentration is to execute and pull the trigger. Occasionally I have seen people come to the range, get ready to shoot, and then freeze when the target is thrown. The stage was set, everyone was ready, the bird flew, everyone waited for the sound of the shot, and then nothing happened. The shooter had all the equipment necessary for the shot, but for some reason the shooter was not able to pull the trigger.

Sometimes we may find ourselves in the same position. We have an area of our life where we sense the leading of the spirit of God. We have done the research, and we have talked to people we trust. We have prayed and feel God is directing us to do something specific. We have even developed the game plan for how we are going to move forward. Then the time comes for us to move, to execute, and we freeze. If this has happened to you, you do not have to feel that you are alone. I believe virtually all of us have at some time or another had this experience happen to us. We are ready, but we do not pull the trigger.

Douglas Vermerren has an article in reliableplant.com which lists reasons people fail to achieve their goals. One of the reasons he cites is the fear of success and/or failure. When it comes time to put our thoughts and plans into action, we are afraid of what the result might be, so we do nothing. We convince ourselves we wouldn't succeed anyway, or we think the result is not worth the effort.

When we look into God's Word we find scriptures which provide us with some perspective about executing what God would have us do. The apostle Paul tells the Philippians they are to continue to work out their salvation with "fear and trembling" for it is actually God who is at work in them to fulfill His good purpose (Philippians 2:12–13). James is talking to fellow Christians about the difference between listening and doing. In verse 22 he tells them, "Do not merely listen to the word, and so deceive yourselves. Do what it says." (James 1:19–27). James continues by instructing the same group of people about faith and works. James says he will show his faith in God by the deeds he does. He goes on to call them foolish for not understanding faith without deeds is useless. James talks about the faith of Abraham and Abraham's obedience in faith. He gives the example of Rahab being considered righteous because of her actions in saving the Hebrew spies (James 2:14–26).

When we look at some of the individuals in God's Word we consider to be examples of Godly men, we find a common trait. These men were men of action even when there was great adversity. Noah built an ark (Genesis 6–7) even when those around him had only thoughts of evil and scoffed at him. On two occasions it is recorded, "Noah did everything just as God commanded. Abraham (formerly Abram) followed God and was the father of the Hebrews (Genesis 12–25). In Genesis 12:4 the following is recorded for us "Abram went, as the Lord had told him." Moses led the Hebrew children out of Egypt. When Moses was wandering in the desert after fleeing Egypt, he saw something he could not understand. He saw a bush that was on fire but not consumed. Moses heard his name being called. Moses went over to the bush and answered God by saying, "here I am." (Exodus 3:4). Joshua was one of the original Hebrew spies and led the Hebrew people into the promised land (Exodus, Numbers, Deuteronomy, Joshua). Elijah was a prophet of God and defeated the prophets of Baal (1 Kings 18–2 Kings 2), King David killed a giant and became a king of God's nation (1 Samuel & 2 Samuel, 1 Kings & 2 Kings, 1 Chronicles & 2 Chronicles). Peter and Paul were leaders of the New Testament church

(Acts). Some of these men had parts of their history which were not God directed. However, each of them followed God and were men of faith and action.

God told the Hebrew children that God will show love to a thousand generations of those who love God and keep his commands (Deuteronomy 5:9–11). On one occasion Jesus was talking to His disciples and gave them this principle: If they love Him they will keep His commandments and He will ask the Father to give them the Holy Spirit and Jesus will love them and show himself to them (John 14:15–21). This principle runs through all Scripture; we have a responsibility to keep the commandments of God and we cannot fulfill our responsibility by being passive. We must take action.

I believe the Bible is clear. It is only by the grace and mercy of God we can be called children of God (Ephesians 2:8). Our salvation is a gift from God. However, God's Word is also clear about the concept of our responsibility. We are to be actively involved in following God's direction. When God instructs us to act, we must execute. Freezing at a time God needs us to step up and perform is not part of God's will for our lives.

Analyze The Results

After I pull the trigger I always want to know if I was successful. When I am on the twenty-five yard range shooting for the half inch or one inch group and the one hundred yard range when I am shooting for the one inch group, I have to get the spotting scope and see where the rounds landed. When I am shooting clay birds I look for each bird to fly apart. If I am shooting doubles in skeet there are times I have to ask my shooting partners if I hit the first bird because I have to quickly transition from shooting the first bird to shooting the second bird.

In all cases I really want to know if I was successful. I analyze the results to see if there are adjustments needed to my form, my stance, the sighting system, or the amount of lead I use at a particular shotgun station. If I was always one hundred percent successful there would be less of a reason to go through the evaluation process. However, I am not close to that level, nor have I ever talked anyone who is one hundred percent successful. I have shot with individuals who shot two perfect rounds of skeet (fifty total birds without a single miss) only to see them fail to hit two birds in a row on the very next round. They were using the same ammunition, same equipment, same field, same birds, everything was the same but obviously something changed. They will often say they started to feel over-confident and stopped concentrating on the fundamentals. They then go back and analyze what went wrong. The point is we are all in the same boat; we need to analyze our actions and make the necessary adjustments.

As we journey through life it is important for us to continually evaluate our behaviors in the light of God's Word. Paul gives a final warning to the church in Corinth. Paul tells them to "Examine yourselves to see whether you are in the faith; test yourselves. Do you not realize Christ Jesus is in you-unless, of course you fail the test." (2 Corinthians 13:5) Paul makes it clear Christ Jesus is not why we fail the test. We cannot blame God for our lack of performance.

There are some things to consider in this scripture. First, we are to examine ourselves. Each of us has the responsibility to evaluate our actions. We can certainly enlist others to provide Godly wisdom and perspective, the wise listen to advice (Proverbs12:15). It is important we listen to others; however, the responsibility to improve is ours. We are supposed to test ourselves. It is not enough to say, "I know what to do." We are to see if our results measure up to what the Scripture says. Paul provides us with the following instruction: We should not deceive ourselves by thinking we are something when we are not. Each of us is to test our own actions and take pride in what we do without comparing ourselves to others (Galatians 6:3–5).

Jesus Christ gives us some specific instruction about who and how we are supposed to analyze. The heading for this section of scripture is

"Judging Others." Jesus is very clear in verses one and two, we are not to judge others and if we do, we will be measured with the same measuring stick (Matthew 7:1–5). The concept here is for each of us to focus on our own performance and not the performance of someone else. When I focus on my own performance and ask for God's guidance, I have found God helps me make corrections, and He does so from a framework of love and not condemnation. God did not send Jesus Christ to condemn us but to save us (John 3:17). God is about our salvation, not our failure.

Jesus asks why we look for the sawdust in our brother's eye when we have a plank in our own eye? If we do not focus on the plank in our own eye Jesus calls us a hypocrite (Matthew 7:3–5). This is an interesting comparison between the two objects in the eyes of the people. One is very small compared to the other. One takeaway from this scripture is there could just be some big planks and maybe sawdust at the same time in our own eye. A secondary takeaway could be we need to first look for the big things in our lives. This is not to say little items are ok, but we need to focus on the big things first. When we focus on the most important things first we can then see the little things more plainly.

A practical example of this could be when we are not sure why our prayer life seems to not be as vibrant and alive as we would have it be. We decide to make a goal around having a better prayer life and include defining the perfect time, location, posture, etc. Those are valid and important questions and need to be evaluated. However, the larger question could be around the following instruction concerning our prayers, "Husbands, in the same way be considerate as you live with your wives, and treat them with respect as the weaker partner and as heirs with you of the gracious gift of life, so that nothing will hinder your prayers." (1 Peter 3:7). The following statement concerning prayer is also something for us to consider, "The prayer of a righteous person is powerful and effective." (James 5:16)

These two scriptures illustrate the concept we need to be most concerned about is a plank issue, not a sawdust issue. The real issue is how do we treat those we love (in this case our wife), and are we striving to be a righteous person? In the Old Testament we see righteousness defined as believing in God (Genesis 15:6), and doing what God commands (Deuteronomy 6:25). In the New Testament we are told we are blessed if we hunger and thirst for righteousness (Matthew 5:6), and our righteousness is given through faith in Jesus Christ to all who believe (Romans 3:2). We always need to make sure the planks are removed before we start looking for the sawdust. I am sure many of us have heard the saying, "we are to be fruit bearers and not fruit inspectors." We need to make sure we are focusing on the planks we own.

As we analyze the results of pulling the trigger, we need to analyze our actions against the fruit of the spirit (Galatians 5:22–23): love, joy peace, patience, kindness, goodness, faithfulness, gentleness and self-control. With God's help we can see where we are doing great and praise God for His help. We can also thank God because He can help us see where we need to make improvements and then He helps us as we make the necessary adjustments. When we are bearing this fruit we can be assured we are hitting the target.

Practice, Practice, Practice

Any of the shooting sports require knowledge of fundamentals of each sport and a base level of equipment to be able to participate. In fact, those things are required for virtually any sport or hobby in which we are involved. The equipment may vary from cameras, golf clubs, firearms, boats, fishing tackle, and a host of other things, but equipment is required nonetheless. Knowledge could include how to select the right golf club for the shot required, the right fishing rod for the type of fish and bait, the right camera and lens combination, firearm ballistics, and other very in-depth details.

Regardless of what we are wanting to accomplish with our targets and our goals, there is a next step required for us to consistently hit our targets.

This step is the one which needs our commitment. That step is; we must practice. It is when we practice our hobby, our craft, our vocation, and I will add our devotion to God, that we start to form habits. Our minds begin to establish the connections required to train our brain and our muscle memory to react to what we are experiencing and then trigger the response we want to have happen. We might make a lucky shot occasionally without practice, but we will not be consistently successful without first consistently practicing our craft. John tells his readers if someone does not continue in the teaching of Christ, the person does not have God (2 John 1:9). This is a description of someone who does not continue to practice what they have learned.

Maxwell Maltz was a plastic surgeon in the 1950's. Dr. Maltz found it took about twenty-one days for patients to get used to their new look. He also found it required a minimum of twenty-one days for the old mental image to disappear and the new one to form. In 1960 Dr. Maltz published his thoughts on behavior change in a book called Psycho-Cybernetics (audiobook). This is how the twenty-one-day rule came into existence.

Phillippa Lilly, Cornelia H.M. Van Jarrsveld, Henry W.W. Potts, and Jane Wardle published a research article titled *How Are Habits Formed: Modeling habit formation in the real world*, first published: 16 July, 2009. The abstract of the article says the time to form a habit ranged from eighteen to 254 days. The study also found missing one opportunity to perform the behavior did not materially affect the habit-forming process. We can miss one chance to hit the target, but we must stay committed to changing our behavior or we will not succeed. Whether the time is eighteen days or all the way to 254 days the message is clear; We cannot do something one time and expect to be successful over the long haul. It takes dedicated repetition and practice for our brains to become trained to respond like we want. Let's look at what this means for our Christian behavior.

In Paul's letter to the Thessalonians, he gives them the following instruction. They are told to "Rejoice always, pray continually, and give thanks in all circumstances; for this is God's will in Christ Jesus." (1 Thessalonians 5:16–18). The words always, continually, and in all things are strong words. They paint a picture of someone who naturally and consistently exhibits these behaviors. This is a picture of someone who has practiced long enough that they do not even have to think to rejoice, pray and give thanks. This has become who they are.

The writer of Hebrews says we are told to "throw off everything that hinders and the sin that so easily entangles us." (Hebrews 12:1–2). We are told to run with perseverance; we are told to fix our eyes on Jesus. Paul talks about straining toward what is ahead (Philippians 3:12–14). These images are of those who continue to run with perseverance, who throw off what hinders them.

Paul tells the believers in Rome the following, "For everything that was written in the past was written to teach us, so that through the endurance taught in the Scriptures and the encouragement they provide we might have hope." (Romans 15:4). Timothy is told to pursue righteousness, Godliness, faith, love, endurance and gentleness (1 Timothy 6:11). Paul is giving thanks because the faith of the church is growing more and more, love for each other is increasing, and they are showing perseverance and faith in persecutions and trials they are enduring (2 Thessalonians 1:3–4). It seems clear we are to continue our walk with God, and endurance and growth are attributes which must be present if we want to live an abundant life.

The reality is, if we want to succeed, we will have to practice what we have learned. It is when we practice that we allow our minds to be renewed. There is no substitute for practice; it is essential.

Thoughts to Consider:

- What are the distractions in my Christian walk?
- On what things do I tend to focus?
- Am I a person of action?
- Do I make it a priority to analyze the results of my actions?
- Could there be a plank in my own eye?
- Am I practicing what I know and have set out to do?
- Am I committed to the life of following Christ?

What Do We Do When We Do Not Hit the Bull's Eye?

Even when we are practicing shooting at our targets it can become frustrating if our progress is slower than we want. It can seem like we will never succeed. I started shooting shotguns about twelve months ago, and I have to admit there have been times when I wondered if I would improve. I kept track of how many shots I had fired from each station; I would compare my results against past outings and hope for any improvement, even if improvement was measured by one more bird hit per round. I would read more, go online and look at videos from 'experts', and listen even harder to the regular guys at the range. I would stand back and try to pick up what they were doing to make it look so easy.

I purchased a shotgun to shoot, and if it wasn't for that purchase, I might have decided the sport was not for me. You know how it goes, "I just don't have the talent, or I can't do that." One day, one of my friends at the range pointed to his head and said something which helped me start to improve. While he still pointed to his head he said, "Galen, it all starts between the ears." I went home that day after a not-so-great outing and thought about what he had said. For me the message was clear; "Was I going to give up or was I going to get my head right?" So…I decided I was going to work on getting my head right. You see, I had to decide to not give up.

The Bible has words for us to consider when we feel like we want to give up. In the Old Testament we see Joshua just after the death of Moses, Joshua's mentor and leader. It finally happened; Moses was dead. God was ready to bring the Israelite children across the Jordon River and into the Promised Land. Joshua was God's chosen leader to take over for Moses. Within the first nine verses of Joshua 1 we see the Lord instructing Joshua three times be strong and courageous. The Lord also told Joshua that, as God was with Moses, God would be with Joshua, and the Lord would not leave Joshua or forsake him. God knew the task would be hard, but God knew Joshua would be able to perform, to hit the target. Joshua knew the task would be hard because he and Caleb had been two of the twelve spies who spied out the land forty years earlier. Joshua and Caleb came back with the report which said the Israelites should enter the Promised Land because God would be with them. The people had said no, and now they were at the same decision point again. In spite of the past Joshua made the decision to go with God.

We are given instructions concerning doing good to all (Galatians 6). It is appropriate for us to consider scripture because sometimes doing good gets old. We just want someone to do something for us. With that as a backdrop, we are told to not become weary in doing the right thing because if we don't give up, we will reap a harvest. This scripture acknowledges we can get weary, but it also points to a harvest.

Paul tells us to be zealous, to keep our spiritual fervor, to serve the Lord, to be joyful in hope, patient in affliction, and faithful in prayer (Romans 12:11–12). This is not a picture of giving up, but of being zealous, fervent, and serving the Lord while being joyful, patient, and faithful. These are words which call us to move forward and not give up. Paul says he has fought the good fight and finished the race and kept the faith (2 Timothy 4:7). We are told to be on our guard, stand firm in faith, be courageous, and be strong (1 Corinthians 16:13). These are but a few of the scriptures in God's word which call us stand firm and not give up. In the last book of the Bible we are told "Whoever has ears, let them hear what the Spirit says to the churches. To the one who is victorious, I will give the right to eat from the tree of life, which is in the paradise of God." (Revelation 2:7) God has called us to be victorious, and He will be with us as we go through our life journey.

It would appear we all have something in common; we all want to succeed. Webster (Merriam-Webster.com) defines 'succeed' in the following way; an intransitive verb meaning to turn out well, to attain a desired object or end. One of the synonyms for succeed is ensue, to commonly suggest a logical consequence of naturally expected development. These definitions are helpful as we examine the dynamics of our human endeavors. The reality is we all have something else in common; we all fail to succeed from time to time.

Let's take a look at some interesting facts from the sports world. Each of the individuals below is a professional in his/her field of endeavor. They were or are the best of the best. These facts can help us put some things in perspective:

- Ty Cobb has the highest MLB lifetime batting average at .366. Some say it may never be duplicated. The other side of the coin is for every hit Ty made he did not get a hit 1.73 times.
- Ed Walsh has the best MLB ERA of 1.816. Again, some say this record will stand forever. However, the record also implies approximately every five innings the opposing team scores an earned run.
- DeAndre Jordon has the best MBA field goal percentage at .6694 percent. This means every third shot DeAndre takes he will miss.
- Drew Brees has the highest NFL pass completion percentage of 74.4 percent. On average, he completes three passes and then fails to complete the next pass.

- Jeff Carter has the highest USBC sanctioned league average of 261.74. This means on the average he had at least one spare in each game he bowled in tournament play.
- Jimmy Connors has won more tennis matches than any other male at 1,274. Jimmy also lost 282 matches, which brings his winning percentage to 82.4 percent.
- In the shotgun game of Sporting Clays a great score is 97 percent, a good score is 85 percent and a respectable score is 75 percent. Just for the record, I am still working on being respectable.

It is a fair statement to say that in any field of endeavor perfection is but a fleeting dream. The reality is there is always room for improvement, something to be unlearned and then relearned, and ways we can be more like what we really want to be. My mentor in marriage education would always say, "we are a process and not a product." I am glad this is true because when I look at past times in my life, I am thankful for areas where there has been improvement.

Jennifer Kunst Ph.D., provides insight into self-improvement and life change when she says, "Nobody Is Perfect, Real change is a self-improvement project build on a foundation of love." She also says, "We can mistakenly believe our limitations and imperfections are obstacles to our mental health, happiness, and peace of mind." "You see, a healthy, happy, and satisfying life is based essentially in love—loving relationships with others, and a loving relationship with ourselves. At its root love has very little to do with perfection."

Jesus provided His followers with an eternal truth when He said they would keep His commandments if they loved Him (John 14:21–23). I have found it is my love for God, my love for my family, and my love for my fellow man which provide the motivation to continue to try again when I miss the target. If I am only interested in me, I will be tempted to say the effort is not worth the result. I have found it is love which helps me even love myself when I have failed and to know God loves me in spite of my humanness. He wants me to grow in Him, but His love for me does not change.

When we miss the target, we need to understand that while we want to succeed, we are going to have moments when we don't get it done. What we do at the point of failure puts us at a crossroad. What we choose to do next has the potential to impact our lives even more than the failure itself.

My wife, our children and I have always enjoyed taking family vacations. We would load up the mini-van and head for the mountains, or the ocean, or both. We would go through the ritual of each person selecting what needed to be loaded into the van. Every year it seemed like the list expanded to include shoes, clothes, food, music, books, and of course the camera equipment. The drill was for everyone to bring 'their stuff' down to the garage, and then I would supervise the big packing event. Most of the time we would be gone seven to ten days so you can picture the size of the pile of stuff. To this day I have not figured out where we put the stuff we picked up during vacation. It seemed every stop the packing required a little more ingenuity, but we were always successful.

We would get loaded up and away we would go with great anticipation as to what the next few days of family togetherness was going to be like. Hiking, eating out, viewing great scenery, singing in the car. We would have a great time enjoying each other and the beautiful world God had given us to experience.

However, I must confess as we approached the time to come back home there were parts of the trip which were starting to be less fun. Packing and unpacking and packing and unpacking seemed to never end. Sometimes there were minor issues which came up but we would always arrive at a compromise and enjoy the day. It was, after all, the family vacation.

One morning after yet another round of unpacking and packing, my family vacation fun meter was probably not as high as it should be. And guess what; an issue arose in the family van on the family vacation and the van driver was not in the mood to compromise. All of a sudden I found myself saying something to my wife, and not in a loving manner. In an instant all the normal family chatter in the van came to an abrupt halt. The only sound was the radio, the engine, and the tires on the pavement. After what seemed like an eternity to me the following came from my children in the back of the van, "Dad, that was rude."

What was I to do? Should I justify my actions and point out how everyone else was wrong? After all, I was the one behind the wheel needing to concentrate on driving. I wanted what I wanted. Maybe I could just ignore the whole situation and hopefully, everyone would forget about the whole event? Let's face it; I had missed the target big time and my children were the ones pointing it out to me. What was I to do?

After realizing I had blown it, there seemed to be only one path to take. I had to apologize to my wife and my children. In the most sincere way I could, I apologized to my wife and children and asked for their forgiveness. They were all gracious and forgave me. However, inside I still felt I had really done a bad thing, and the reality was, I had.

You see, I was at the point some of us get to when we have missed the target and don't know why. We have several choices to make. Do we listen to the devil and get stuck in self-pity? Do we ruminate about the situation until we convince ourselves the situation is totally the fault of someone else? Do we decide we are never going to put ourselves in that situation again and withdraw from those around us? Or do we look to God, confess our failing, and then allow God to comfort us and empower us to try again. I feel this is probably more a function of the human condition than we want to admit, so let's look at what we can learn about handling missing our targets, and our failures in life.

My wife and I have been privileged to be involved in marriage ministry for more than thirty years. We have read many books about the marriage relationship and have taken training from professionals in marriage relationships. We have led book studies, retreats, and facilitated marriage education programs. All of this has helped and continues to help our relationship grow into an abundant, fulfilled marriage. The concepts we have learned and continue to practice help us minimize mistakes and recognize how to address points of failure when they occur.

In the book, A Lasting Promise The Christian Guide to Fighting for Your Marriage, Scott Stanley talks about the three keys for building and keeping a strong and happy marriage. On page 51 he shares the following keys: decide don't slide, do your part, and make it safe to connect. I want us to look at two of these keys as they relate to what we do when we miss the target.

The first key is 'Decide don't slide' p.51-54. The principle behind this key is that we must make a conscious decision to do what we know is right as opposed to sliding into other behaviors. Our normal behaviors can be brought about because of a habit we have established. For example, when I feel stressed, I withdraw and don't want to talk about the issue. I might yell because I can 'get it out'. Sometimes we slide because we are influenced by our culture, our family of origin, our friends, or a whole host of other things which can influence us. The problem is when we slide, we will almost always fail to handle the situation better. Sometimes we slide because we believe it is the easy way out. When we choose to slide, we don't pull the trigger and we don't even try, not to mention missing the target.

The second key is 'Do your part' p.55-57. The principle here is that individually we are responsible for doing what we know is right. When confronted with a choice to make as to how we are going to act or react, we have to understand, regardless of the expected response or actual response of the other person, we have to do our part. One example of this is Matthew 6:14–15 where we are told God will forgive us if we forgive others, and if we don't forgive others God will not forgive us. In this situation we simply do not have an option. We are to do our part, which is to forgive. When we rely on others to do for us what we can only do for ourselves, we miss the target.

Let's look at two examples in the Old Testament where individuals failed. When the individuals realized their failure, they had choices to make; the choices they made led to more failure and ultimately those decisions ended up having long lasting and disastrous impacts. We are going to look at a famous father and a famous son through the lens of failure and how failure was addressed.

The first example we will examine is King David and Bathsheba (2 Samuel 11–12). David was born around 1000 BCE. David was the youngest of eight sons of Jesse from Bethlehem. David also had two half-sisters. Prior to becoming King, David was a shepherd and a musician.

We have likely all heard the story of David and Goliath (1 Samuel 17). Goliath was over nine and a half feet tall, and his armor weighed approximately 125 pounds. Goliath would taunt the army of Saul and ask to fight a single solider with the winner of the fight determining the victory for the army. David came in the name of the Lord, a sling and five smooth stones in his pouch, approached Goliath, and killed Goliath with the sling and one stone. David become a friend of King Saul and a good friend of Jonathan, the son of King Saul. King Saul rejected the instruction of God and eventually David became king when David was thirty years old. It is at this point in David's life we read the account of David and Bathsheba.

It was spring and we find David at home, in the palace. The Bible says this was the time when the kings went to war. Instead of going to war, David sent Joab and the Israelite army to destroy the Ammonites. Joab was the nephew of David and the commander of the army. It was David's responsibility to lead the army into battle. Not only was David not leading the battle or praying to God to provide for the victory of his army, he was getting out of bed after taking a nice afternoon nap.

David took a stroll on the roof and saw a beautiful woman, Bathsheba. David was curious and sent servants to find out about the woman. David then sent messengers to have Bathsheba brought to the palace where David had sex with her. David sent Bathsheba back to her home. Sometime later Bathsheba realized she was pregnant and sent this information to David. It is interesting to note that prior to having sex with David, Bathsheba had just completed the purification process required after her menstrual cycle. Bathsheba's husband, Uriah, was away at war (where David should have been), so there was no doubt as to who was the father of the child.

David began the process of trying to get Uriah back to Uriah's house so Uriah would sleep with Bathsheba and no one would be the wiser. David summoned Uriah to the palace. On two different occasions David tried to get Uriah to go home to Bathsheba but on each occasion Uriah stayed at the palace entrance. Uriah would not go home and 'wine and dine' while his fellow soldiers were at war with the enemies of Israel.

David then set in motion a plan to have Uriah die in battle. David instructed Joab to place Uriah in the front of the battle, where the battle was the fiercest. Joab was to have the other soldiers pull back so Uriah would be exposed and Uriah would surely be killed. Joab obeyed David, executed the plan, and Uriah was killed. Joab sent a message back to David stating the battle was fierce, the troops had to pull back, but Uriah was dead. In response to Joab's message we find one of the most disturbing statements ever made by David. David replied, "Well, tell Joab not to be discouraged." "The sword kills one as well as the other! Fight harder next time, and conquer the city!" (2 Samuel 11:25 NLT)

When Bathsheba completed her time of mourning, David sent for her and brought her into the palace and she became one of his wives. David's actions were not looked on with favor from the Lord, "But the thing David had done displeased the Lord." (2 Samuel 11:27). Approximately one year later Nathan, the prophet of God, confronted David and told David a story about two men. One man was poor and one was rich. The rich man owned many sheep and cattle, and the poor man owned one little lamb. The poor man had worked hard to buy the little lamb, he raised the little lamb and it grew up with his children. The poor man fed the lamb from his own cup and plate. The poor man cuddled the little lamb like a baby daughter. One day a guest arrived at the house of the rich man. The rich man wanted to feed his guest. The rich man decided instead of having one of his own flock killed and served, he would take the little lamb from the poor man, kill it, and serve it to his guest.

When David heard the story he was furious. David said, "As surely as the Lord lives," he vowed, "any man who would do such a thing deserves to die!" David went on to say the rich man must repay four lambs to the poor man. Then Nathan said to David, "You are the man!" After Nathan gave David more information David replied, "I have sinned against the Lord." Nathan told David the Lord had forgiven David and David would not die for the sin.

Nathan went on to tell David that because of his actions the sword would not depart from David's household. David's wives would be given to his companion before David's eyes. David's punishment would be for all of Israel to see in the daylight. David had given occasion for the enemies of the Lord to blaspheme, and lastly, his child would die.

It is important to realize David's actions came years after David was described by Samuel as a man after the heart of God and years after the victory of David over Goliath. I believe David's sin might be the most horrific of any recorded in the Old Testament. The account has many failures embedded in it. The first was David neglected his duty; he should have been off to war. He missed the target. He should have been seeking God's face; he was napping in the palace and then checking out the surroundings. He missed the target. He should have turned the other way when he saw Bathsheba but he eventually committed adultery. He missed the target.

David planned the murder of an innocent person; he should have been seeking God's forgiveness. He missed the target. David should have had some sense of remorse prior to Nathan confronting David, but one year after the event David showed no remorse. He missed the target. David had no compassion and understanding for what he asked Bathsheba and Joab to do; he used them for his own desires. He missed the target. At every step in the progression of David's actions he should have realized his failure and made the necessary corrections so the consequences of those actions would not build on each other and lead to a disastrous outcome. He failed to analyze the results. The outcome of David's actions impacted him personally, his family, and ultimately the nation of Israel.

If we only focus on what David did wrong, missing the target and his failures, we can wonder if there is any hope. The good news is the rest of the story, God's forgiveness of David. We need to look no farther than Psalms 51 to see the words David penned concerning the events we have examined. In the first two verses we see David asking God to have mercy on him according to the unfailing love and great compassion of God. David asks God to wash away all his iniquity and cleanse him from sin. In the rest of the verses we see David ask for God to cleanse him and make him whiter than snow, to have David's bones rejoice, and to blot out all of David's iniquity. David goes on to say, "My sacrifice, O God, is a broken spirit; a broken and contrite heart you, God, will not despise." (Psalms 51:17).

It is important to realize we do not have to be defined by our mistakes, our failures, or our sins. To illustrate this point all we have to do is to take another look at the life of King David. David like many of the Old Testament heroes had one or more serious character flaws. In David's case, there was sin at the lowest of human levels. David was an adulterer and a murderer. Under the Mosaic system of law, the punishment for these sins was death. Yet we look at David as the boy who followed God and slew the giant Goliath. In fact, virtually every children's program about David in church will often refer to David, the giant killer.

David was the second King of Israel. David wrote some of the best poetry of his day, if not of all time, and is credited with writing at least seventy-three of the psalms in the book of Psalms. The Twenty-Third Psalm is one of the scriptures many learn at a relatively early age. Perhaps one of the most interesting aspects concerning David is that multiple times in the New Testament Jesus is referred to as the Son of David. In Luke 1 verses twenty-six through thirty-eight we have the angel Gabriel talking with Mary the mother of Jesus. In this passage Gabriel says, "The Lord God will give him the throne of his father David." (Luke 1:32).

The point for us to understand is this; David was not defined by his great sin with Bathsheba and Uriah. Instead, he has a revered place in religious history and God continues to use him even in our time almost 3,000 years later through the psalms David wrote. Many of us find comfort from reading those words David penned so many years ago. We can feel his passion for truly being a man after God's heart.

The second example we will examine is one of the failings of Solomon. Solomon is also called Jeddah in the Old Testament and the Hebrew bible. Solomon was the tenth son of King David and the second son of Bathsheba. While Solomon was king, he controlled the trade routes coming out of Edom, Arabia, India, Africa, and Judaea. One of the ways he accomplished this was by having alliances, which were strengthened by having 700 wives of royal birth and 300 concubines. He purportedly built the first temple of God in Jerusalem. He was approximately eighty years old when he died. As a young man Solomon acknowledged he needed wisdom to be king of Israel, so one of the first things Solomon did as king was to ask God for wisdom. Solomon started out on the right track (2 Chronicles 1).

In chapter 11 of 1 Kings, we find the account of Solomon's wives and how those wives led to his demise. When the Hebrew children were getting ready to enter the Promised Land, they were given specific instructions by Moses (Deuteronomy 7:3–4) to not intermarry with the people of the land they were going to occupy. The reason was the non-Hebrew people would turn the Hebrew people away from following God. The Hebrew children would follow other gods, the anger of the Lord would be kindled, and He would destroy the Hebrew people. Solomon would have been very familiar with the command.

Solomon chose to not do his part in following the commands of God. Instead of remaining true to the instructions given by God, Solomon decided to behave in direct opposition to God's commands. In 1 Kings. 11:4–13 we find an interesting dynamic about how Solomon's life changed. The scripture says "as Solomon grew old his wives turned his heart after other gods and he was not fully devoted to the Lord God, as the heart of David his father had been." (1 Kings, 11:4). This would indicate the turning of Solomon's heart was not an immediate change. The change happened after years of Solomon not doing his part in following the leadership of God.

When Solomon aged, he built high places for the burning of incense and offering of sacrifices to the gods of his wives. Solomon's failure to keep God's covenant and commands caused God to take the kingdom away from Solomon. God did say for the sake of David, God would not take the kingdom away in Solomon's lifetime, but it would happen in the lifetime of Solomon's son. For the sake of David, God's servant, and Jerusalem there would be one tribe left in the kingdom. In 1 Kings Chapter 12 we see the split of the kingdom, with the kingdom never to be united again. Solomon's decision to not do his part led to the end of a united kingdom and set the stage for the eventual exile of the children of Israel.

In the New Testament we are given some direction and promises concerning the actions we need to take when we miss the target. God's word tells us if we confess our sins, God is faithful and just to forgive our sins. This is a wonderful promise which can help us allow God to take away the guilt and shame which comes from our failure to hit the target. The rest of the verse in also important for us to examine. It says that He can "purify us from all unrighteousness." (1 John 1:9). This means God can help us as we attempt to hit the target again. He can help us with what needs to be done differently to enable us to hit the target.

We also find the following words, "My dear children, I write this to you so that you will not sin. But if anybody does sin, we have an advocate with the Father—Jesus Christ, the Righteous One. Jesus is the atoning sacrifice for our sins, and not only for ours but also for the sins of the whole world." (1 John 2:1). Jesus was the very Son of God, but Jesus was also human just like you and me, He understands what it is like for us to live our lives. We have a high priest who can empathize with our weakness because Jesus was tempted in every way, just like us, and even through those temptations Jesus did not sin (Hebrews 4:15). We can trust God's word and realize when we miss the target, we are not left alone. Jesus, through the presence of the Holy Spirit, is by our side and we can go to Him for the forgiveness, comfort, and the strength required to move forward.

When we look at Hebrews 12:4–13 we see spiritual teaching about discipline and what discipline can produce in our lives. We know that no discipline seems pleasant at the time; in fact, it may be painful. However, there is more to the teaching. If we allow ourselves to be taught, discipline can produce a harvest of righteousness and peace (Hebrews 12:11). In the New Living Translation (NLT) the result of this discipline will be a "peaceful harvest of right living." (Hebrews 12:11 NLT) God's word has promised to help us learn from our mistakes and to help us move forward in our life.

Paul tells us when we are in Christ, we are a new creation. The old self is gone, and we are now part of God's new creation (2 Corinthians 5:17). The Message version of the Bible states it this way, "Now we look inside, and what we see is that anyone united with the Messiah gets a fresh start, is created new. The old life is gone; a new life burgeons! Look at it!" (2 Corinthians 5:17 MSG)

The devil lies and says we are not worthy of God's forgiveness, and we have failed beyond the ability of God to forgive. When we have these thoughts, we need to remember they come from the devil and not God. We know the devil is the father of lies (John 8:44). We know God loves us, so when we have thoughts that we are not loved, we can rest assured these thoughts are coming from the devil and not God.

Our reality is this—because we are children of God and have accepted

Jesus Christ as our Savior, we can go through this life with a different way of viewing things and a different way of dealing with missing the target. Even when we miss the target, when we fail, when we sin, we have the promise that God is faithful. God is in the business of forgiving us and empowering us to try again. With God's help we can continue to take another shot at the target. When we continue to make our best effort and allow God to lead us where God wants us to go, we can say with David, "The Lord is my light and my salvation—so why should I be afraid? The Lord protects me from danger—so why should I tremble?" (Psalms 27:1 NLT)

Thoughts to Consider:

- What is my first response when I am not totally successful?
- What are some things which sometimes cause me to want to give up?
- Do I expect perfection in every situation I encounter?
- What do I tend to do first when I fail?
- Do I let myself slide into behaviors which are not what God would have me do?
- Do I feel defined by my mistakes?
- Is there anything I am allowing to turn my heart away from God?
- Am I allowing myself to believe the lies of the devil?
- Do I believe God is faithful to forgive me when I confess my sin?

Conclusion

I started this project with the intention of leaving future generations of my family with my perspective of what my responsibility is to live the abundant Christian life. I hope and pray the thoughts brought forward in this book can be helpful in enabling them to set and hit the targets required for them to experience their own abundant life. We have looked at many different aspects of what it means to have targets to aim for in our walk with God. We have looked at the steps required to hit the target and we have discussed what we need to do when we miss the target. Now I want to look at some final thoughts and hopefully tie things together.

One time I prepared a talk titled "Doing Your Part" for a Christian men's group. We defined the phrase this way; "do" means to bring to pass, carry out, perform, execute; "your" means of or relating to oneself; "part" means an essential portion or integral element. When the phrase is put together it could be stated as follows- I must execute everything which is within my responsibility to perform the essential elements of what I am striving to accomplish.

In the preparation for the talk I found the word "if" is used 1,784 times in 1,589 verses within the NIV. Many of these instances are with conditional promises. Examples include the following: If my people will... (2 Chronicles 7:14), If you remain in me and I remain in you… (John

15:5); If you love me you will…(John 14:15). The objective of the talk was to help men understand as Christ followers we have responsibilities to do our part. We can't just sit and wait for God to do all the work.

I believe is it vitally important at the end of the day to realize we are the ones who tune the radio; we pick the stations with the remote. We are the ones who cook the meals and go to work every day. God doesn't grasp the steering wheel of our car: we steer the car ourselves. We are the ones who make the final decisions concerning what we will allow to come into our body, our heart, and our mind. We are the ones who decide if we are going to 'decide and not slide' when the next decision point comes. We are the ones who make the decision to 'do our part' when it would be easier to step back. I want my children, grandchildren and future generations to understand they have a responsibility to do the right thing, to follow what God's Word has instructed them to do.

If we profess to be Christ followers, we can't claim ignorance as to what we must do to live a Godly life. In 2 Peter 1:3–10 we find instructions under the heading of "Confirming One's Calling and Election". This is an incredibly rich passage which tells us God's divine power has given us everything we need to live a Godly life. This comes about because of our knowledge of Jesus. We have been given great and precious promises with the express purpose being that we participate in the divine nature of God. Because of this participation we can escape the corruption of this world which is caused by our evil desires. We are then told to make every effort to become like Christ and in an increasing measure. These qualities will help us be effective and productive for Jesus. We are told if we don't have these qualities, we are nearsighted and blind. We are told again to make every effort to confirm our calling and election. If we practice these behaviors, we will never stumble and we will receive a rich welcome into God's eternal kingdom.

So, if we do choose to obey God, what can the abundant life look like? I believe one attribute is peace. David tells us (Psalms 37:4) to take delight in the Lord and the Lord will give us the desires of our heart. In Matthew 11:28–30 Jesus tells all who are weary and burdened to come to Him and He will give them rest. In John 14:27 we are told Jesus gives us peace the world can't give so we are to not let our hearts be troubled or afraid.

We have incredible promises which help us know we are not alone as we walk through life. We find some wonderful words of encouragement in the fourteenth chapter of John. "And I will ask the Father, and he will give you an advocate to help you and be with you forever—the Spirit of Truth." Jesus goes on to say the Spirit will be with us and live in us. (John 14:16–17). He continues with the following, "Whoever has my commands and keeps them is the one who loves me. The one who loves me will be loved by my Father, and I too will love them and show myself to them." (John 14:21). Verse 23 restates the same common theme. We do not need to despair because God and Jesus through the presence of the Holy Spirit will make their home in us. We have instant access to God.

Paul talks about Life Through the Spirit and Present Suffering and Future Glory (Romans 8:1–30). We are told the Spirit helps us in our weakness (Romans 8:26). When we don't know how to pray the Spirit himself intercedes for us. Even when we are weak we are not powerless. We have the Spirit to walk with us. It is because of the life through the Spirit and the promise in all things God works for the good for those who love Him (Romans 8:28). Paul ends the chapter by saying we are more than conquerors. Paul says there is nothing that can separate us from the love of God which is in Christ Jesus our Lord. We do not have to go through life with a defeated attitude. God is for us and with us.

All these words provide comfort and hope as we go through this life. They are, however, easier to say when things are going well than when we are truly in a battle. It is in those times of battle when we put our faith in God to the test.

Tonight (11/09/20) as I sit and review these words there are 50,800,000 coronavirus cases in the world, there have been 1,260,000 deaths and

33,200,000 cases of recovered individuals. World-wide the numbers are continuing to climb. The world economy is taking a significant hit. People are afraid. What does this have to do with us obeying God? While I don't have the knowledge or resources to cure the problem, I do have the words of Christ to provide comfort to me and those I come in contact with. Jesus Christ says the following, "*I have told you these things, so that in me you may have peace. In this world you will have trouble. But take heart! I have overcome the world.*" (John 16:33). By our faith in Jesus, we can have peace in the midst of the storm. The point is this: we must make the decision to have faith and to trust the promises God provides.

There is one final personal experience and perspective I want to leave with you. If there is any good which comes in the sharing of this experience, the good belongs to God, our creator, who loves us more than we can even comprehend and who wants us to live an abundant life with Him at the controls.

I grew up living in rural central Missouri. This was in the country with no plumbing for eight years, wood heat and no air conditioning. I lived in that environment from my fifth birthday in 1958 until my seventeenth birthday. My parents and I lived a quarter of a mile down the road from my grandparents. My grandparents owned some land, raised some cattle, milked some cows by hand for a while and then installed the 'milking machine.' What an invention! My grandfather let me sit on his lap and drive the tractor. My grandfather also had a small sawmill. Eventually my father bought the sawmill and on the weekends and every summer I worked there with my dad. I started working at the mill when I was nine. Life was good. Working with my Dad helped me develop a strong body, a strong work ethic and helped me to learn how to solve problems. We went to church in town (forty-five minutes away) on Sunday morning, Sunday evening and Wednesday night.

I went to the same grade school my father went to with the same first grade teacher. There were nine students in my class, and we had two grades in the same room with the same teacher. When it was time for me to go to high school my parents said they wanted me to go to a different high school because of the opportunities available at the new school. My distant cousin went to the same school so I thought it would be fun. I went to a high school which was out of my normal school district. I was 'out of district' so I could not play sports my freshman year. I practiced with the basketball team but was not on any team and did not go to any games as a participant.

In my sophomore year the football coach approached me in the hall on the first day of school and said, "You are going to play football." I informed the coach that I had not touched a football in my life and didn't know the first thing about the game, to which he replied, "That's ok, you will be a lineman and I will teach all you need to know." So, off I went on my new adventure. I was already two weeks behind the team in terms of conditioning because I had not attended the 'two-a-days'. I did find working at the sawmill had prepared me for some of the 'fun' I was experiencing in practice, and I thought, "Hey, I think I like this."

Playing football was a great experience. We were a small school in rural Missouri, part of a small conference. I had some success and was all conference defensive end and second string all conference offensive guard my senior year. From then on I have always been reasonably active. I played racquetball, basketball, water volleyball, jumped rope and jogged until the knees said stop. I found I could continue to ride my bicycle and my knees didn't seem to complain much.

I came to Kansas City to attend electronics school. I went to work at a local company and began to move to different jobs at the company. I met my future wife at church, and we married in 1977. She was and continues to be the love of my life, my best friend, and my spiritual hero. Along the way we were blessed with three great children. Even though I intellectually knew bad things happen to good people, our immediate family had been spared any truly catastrophic issues. The birth of our son was scary, but that was now twelve years in the past and life was very good!

This brings us to the fall of 2003. We lived by a great bicycle trail, and I was riding my bicycle about sixty or more miles per week. I began to notice some discomfort in my lower abdomen and I thought it was just due to the bicycle. I changed seats on the bicycle and the discomfort did not go away. I started seeing a urologist and in early 2004 the testing began. Medicine, ultrasounds, scopes, and then eventually a biopsy was ordered. During all this time my anxiety level was low because I thought the discomfort was just exercise related. I was fifty-one years old at the time and the bodies of fifty-one-year-old men don't work like twenty-one-year-old bodies. I had been a Christian since I was nine, and I knew Christians sometimes get off easy; that thought was somewhere back there in the corner of my mind.

Then came the day my wife and I went to see the doctor and get the results of the biopsy. In my mind I was still thinking this would be a 'sports thing.' We were directed to a small exam room and sat down. In a very few minutes the door opened, the doctor came in, shook our hands, sat down in the chair and said, "I have the results of the biopsy and I need to let you know they are positive. You have prostate cancer." The doctor helped us understand the treatment options available at the time and told us to go home and take some time to research and discuss those treatment options with each other. We then made an appointment to meet with the doctor again and decide on the next steps. We left the doctor's office, went to our car, held each other and began to cry. At that moment in time my life changed and a new step in my Christian journey began.

I began to go through the grief cycle (Five Stages of Grief, by Elisabeth Kubler Ross & David Kessler). The stages are denial, anger, bargaining, depression and acceptance. I quickly went through the denial stage. I am a "numbers" guy. I had the results from the doctor in my hand, this situation was real; it was happening to me. Did I get angry? You bet I did. I am not proud of that fact but I would not be telling truth if I said I didn't. "God, why did you let this happen?"

It was at this time the devil started to do some serious work in my head. I started to wonder about this Christian thing. I mean after all, my wife and I had always practiced tithing (amazing how we are tempted to go there first), we were teachers in Sunday school, I was on the church board, and my wife played piano at church. We were actively involved in the marriage ministry at our local church as well giving marriage enrichment retreats for other churches. We were actively involved in the lives of our family of three children, the oldest two being in college in another state and our twelve-year-old son still at home. We were attempting to show them what it means to grow up loving and serving God and we were trying to help them understand that their experience with God must be their own. We had been doing all the Christian stuff. We had responsibilities. Why should this happen to us? I knew then these thoughts were not from God, but I still had them, and I had to deal with them. We asked for people to pray for our situation, and we started on a new faith journey. I spent time praying specifically about our situation and wanting to feel the peace of God in my spirit.

On a very early spring day I was spending time sitting on the deck, reading God's word, praying with all my heart, and trying to listen to what God wanted to tell me in the middle of this situation. I remember asking God this question, "God, is this what an abundant life is supposed to look like? Does it look like possibly dying of cancer when I am fifty-one and leaving my wife to raise our twelve-year-old son?"

It was at that moment in time I felt impressed in my spirit to do the following. I was supposed to pick up a pencil and a note card and write. I went inside, got a pencil and note card, went back outside and sat down in my chair on the deck. I asked God what I was supposed to write. I felt in my spirit I was supposed to write some of the things I had experienced in my life, so I started to write. As I began to write I realized the thoughts weren't necessarily in order of importance, I also realized I was not needing to think about what to write, I was just writing down what was coming to my mind. I realized every item on the list was significant to me. The thoughts stopped and I stopped writing. I still have the note card and here is what it has on it in the order I wrote the items:

Things I have experienced:

- The love of a woman
- Children
- Messing up
- Being made whole
- Climbing a mountain
- Forgiveness
- Warm sand on the beach
- Sunset over the ocean
- Good job well done
- Graduation days
- A tiny hand grasping my finger
- Peace from God
- Moonlit nights
- The sound of rain on a tin roof
- A relaxing vacation
- The voice of a wise man
- A beautiful picture
- The sound of a child's laugh
- The thrill of victory
- The voice of a friend in a time of trouble

When I finished writing the list I just sat and tried as intently as I knew how to listen to God. I did not hear an audible voice but I will always believe the Holy Spirit of God planted the next thought into my mind. The thought was this, "Galen, I believe that looks like a very abundant life to me."

You see, it was then that I started moving away from listening to the devil, from dealing with denial, from anger, from bargaining, and from depression. I started the process of moving to acceptance. This doesn't mean the devil went away. He was around to try and fill my mind with his lies. When lies from him would come into my brain I would recall scriptures which were meaningful to me. I would still have times when I would slip back into the previous stages of grief. When I became aware of the slippage of my thoughts I would recall scriptures to mind and then look at the note card I had written that day on the deck.

For me, acceptance was comprised of multiple facets of the cancer situation and also many areas of my spiritual life. It included my theology, my understanding of God and how I fit into His plan. I remember going through the following items in my mind while sitting on the deck.

The first thing I had to accept was that God had been with me before I was ever born and He knew all about me. My current situation was not a surprise to Him. I had to accept that just because I was a Christian there was no pass on the unpleasant stuff of life. I had to realize I lived in a fallen world, with those consequences at play in my part of the world. The promises of God for me were; He had always loved me, currently loved me, and would always love me. He had promised to be with me forever which included all my days, not just those prior to cancer. I had to accept His ways were above my ways and there would be things I would never be able to figure out.

Maybe the most important thing was for me to realize was I was His creation, created for Him to use for His glory. My life was about Him and not me. That day on the deck God helped me realize I was living the abundant life, and He was faithful to walk with me regardless of what happened with the cancer thing.

It has been sixteen years since I sat on the deck one early spring day and got to the point where I listened to what I will always believe was the Holy Spirit witnessing to my spirit. The doctor, my wife, and I agreed on a treatment for the cancer and I have been cancer free since May of 2004. There have been other times in my life when I have realized I either decide to choose to believe God's word or I don't, when I have realized the choice is up to me and no one else, but I must say, there have not been any other days when I was more keenly aware of that fact than early spring in 2004. In a very real sense this experience helped put my thinking on a different path and hopefully the path of a more mature follower of Christ.

Lots of things have happened since then. There have been times of great sorrow and loss when dear family and friends have made the transition from this earth to their eternal home with God. There have been times of intense joy, having new sons-in-law and a daughter-in-law enter the family and the addition of five grandchildren to the family. Grandchildren have asked God to come live in their heart. All these things have contributed to the tapestry which makes up my life.

When I look at my life, I must say I have found God's word to be true. There is no substitute for the wisdom and love of God. He made us, knows us, and has promised to be with us forever. He truly wants to give us an abundant life. My prayer is that all of us strive to do our part to bring glory to God in everything we do. In the words of my mentor, "just get up every morning, pray you will please God in what you do today, and then be alert to what God brings into your life."

My favorite hymn is, "It Is Well With My Soul," by Horatio G Spafford in 1873. The hymn was written after tragic events in Spafford's life. His four-year-old son was killed in the Great Chicago Fire of 1871. He suffered financial setbacks due the fire and his business interests were further impacted by the economic downtown of 1873. He planned to take his family to Europe on the SS Ville du Havre but because of a late change of plans he sent them ahead. During the crossing the ship, after a collision with the Loch Earn, another sea vessel, all four of Spafford's daughters died. His wife survived and sent him a telegram with these words, "Saved alone…" He penned the words to the hymn as his ship passed where his daughters died. I would ask you to think about the situations Horatio had experienced and yet he could write the words of this wonderful hymn.

To my family and anyone else who should happen to read this book I want to leave you with these words from the hymn and words from our Lord Jesus Christ. I know regardless of the situations we face, God loves us, and He is faithful. All praise to God.

It Is Well with My Soul
Horatio G. Spa Ford, 1873
Public Domain

When peace, like a river, attendeth my way,
When sorrows like a sea billows roll;
Whatever my lot, Thou has taught me to say,
It is well, it is well with my soul

Refrain:
It is well with my soul,
It is well, it is well with my soul.

Though Satan should buffet, though trials should come,
Let this blest assurance control,
That Christ has regarded my helpless estate,
And hath shed His own blood for my soul.

My sin—oh, the bliss of this glorious thought!—
My sin, not in part but the whole,
Is nailed to the cross, and I bear it no more,
Praise the Lord, praise the Lord, O my soul!

But, Lord, 'tis for Thee, for Thy coming we wait,
The sky, not the grave, is our goal;

Oh, trump of the angel! Oh, voice of the Lord!
Blessed hope, blessed rest of my soul!

And Lord, hast the day when the faith shall be sight,
The clouds be rolled back as a scroll;
The trump shall resound, and the Lord shall descend,
Even so, it is well with my soul.

"The thief comes only to steal and kill and destroy; I have come that they may have life, and have it to the full." (John 10:10)

"I have told you these things, so that in me you may have peace. In this world you will have trouble. But take heart! I have overcome the world." (John 16:33)

Thoughts to Consider:

- How can I allow God to comfort me in times of sorrow and stress?
- What does the abundant life look like to me?
- What things do I need to accept as the facts of my current situation?
- Do I choose to believe God's word for me?
- Does my thinking need to be on a different path?
- God is faithful—I can trust Him.

Chapter Index

1. Introduction

2. The Battle Starts in the Mind

3. God's Will, Can We Know It?

4. What Is the Abundant Life?

10. Let's Get in the Game and Pull The Trigger

11. What Do We Do When We Don't Hit the Bulls' Eye?

12. Conclusion

Scripture Index

Old Testament

New Testament

Other Resources Index

Printed in the United States
By Bookmasters